THE FIRST TRIAL OF
MARY, QUEEN OF SCOTS

The First Trial of Mary, Queen of Scots

Gordon Donaldson

Professor of Scottish History
University of Edinburgh

NEW ENGLISH LIBRARY
TIMES MIRROR

First published in Great Britain by B. T. Batsford Ltd., 1969
© Gordon Donaldson, 1969

*

FIRST NEL PAPERBACK EDITION MAY 1974

*

NEL Books are published by
New English Library Limited from Barnard's Inn, Holborn, London E.C.1.
Made and printed in Great Britain by Hunt Barnard Printing Ltd., Aylesbury, Bucks.

45001933 0

ACKNOWLEDGMENT

The quotation on pages 168–9 is taken from Eric Linklater
Mary Queen of Scots (D. Dobson, 1952)

Contents

Preface

The better-known trial of Mary, Queen of Scots, took place at the end of 1586 and led to her condemnation and to her execution at Fotheringhay in February 1587. The crime for which she was then tried and found guilty was complicity in plots against the life of Queen Elizabeth. But Mary had been tried before, shortly after she arrived in England as a refugee in 1568. The crime of which she had been accused was complicity in the murder of her second husband, Lord Darnley. The verdict was, in effect, 'Not proven', and no sentence was pronounced, but the punishment she incurred was life imprisonment.

It could not be said that any phase or aspect of Queen Mary's life has been neglected, but what can be called her first trial has received less attention than most parts of her career. The evidence produced at the investigation has, indeed, been much used in discussions of the authenticity of the Casket Letters and the responsibility for the murder of Darnley, but the proceedings have been little studied for their own sake. They fall, of course, at something of a watershed in Mary's biography. The girl in France, the romantic young Queen in Scotland, on one side: on the other, the prematurely ageing captive, the royal martyr – even if only a martyr to rheumatism, as Josephine Tey suggested – these are all too familiar. But the Mary of 1568-9 – a fugitive from justice as a suspected adulteress and murderess, her life in peril from her own subjects, yet bent on vengeance, ready to abandon Bothwell for whom she had given up so much, ready too to enter on a flirtation with Anglicanism as a condition of her restoration – this is in some ways a less attractive figure. But it is not less fascinating, for there could be much debate on the question whether Mary's behaviour at this stage is consistent or inconsistent with her conduct earlier and later.

The investigations which dragged on for months, first at York, then at Westminster and finally at Hampton Court, made a show of impartiality between Mary and her rebellious subjects, but stage by stage took on the character of an enquiry into Mary's alleged guilt. Yet there was an air of unreality about the formal proceedings. It would not be true to say that nobody cared much whether Mary should be judicially proved innocent or guilty, but it is true that nobody cared much whether she really was innocent or guilty. Essentially, each party – the English government, Mary's supporters, Mary's accusers – were concerned to exploit the situation for their own ends. Political considerations dominated, and if any of those who were involved had notions of justice in the abstract they said remarkably little about them. The question of punishing Mary as a criminal, should she be found guilty, was never seriously faced, and the possibility of setting her at liberty unconditionally should she be found innocent was, equally, never entertained. The question was a political one – should she or should she not be restored to her throne?

This fact makes it more important to deal at some length with the antecedents and the consequences of the formal proceedings. The first two chapters therefore deal with the events in Mary's earlier life which throw light on her character and policy, and which shaped the attitude of contemporaries towards her. The third chapter attempts to analyse the considerations which influenced the parties present at the inquiry and which perhaps did more than any of the formal proceedings to determine the ultimate outcome. Chapter 7 explains how a decision was reached for political reasons rather than on the strength of the evidence which had emerged in the course of the investigation, and the final chapter deals briefly with Mary's life in captivity and the events which led to its fatal conclusion.

The labours of anyone who writes about Mary may be complicated by the many theories put forward in the past, but they are immensely lightened by the diligence of those earlier scholars who have systematically assembled the source material. Thus, the documentation for nearly everything recounted in chapters 1 and 2 of the present book is to be found in David Hay Fleming, *Mary, Queen of Scots*, 2nd edn, 1898. Some of my own views of Mary and my speculations about the Kirk o' Field mystery have already been printed, with references to sources, in *Scotland: James V to James VII*, 1956, and, more briefly, in *Scottish Kings*, 1967. For the enquiry itself, most of the material is calendared in *Calendar of State Papers relating to Scotland and Mary, Queen of Scots*, vol. ii, and in the Historial MSS. Commission *Report on the MSS. of the Marquis of Salisbury*, vol. i. A large number of the items included in these calendars, along with others not so included, are printed in full in Walter Goodall, *An Examination of the Letters said to be written by Mary, Queen of Scots, to James, Earl of Bothwell*, 2 vols, 1754. Several of the Salisbury, or Cecil, papers are printed in full in Samuel Haynes and William Murdin, *Collection of State Papers . . . left by Cecil, Lord Burghley*, 1740, 1759. A selection of some of the more significant documents has recently been printed by M. H. Armstrong Davison in *The Casket Letters*, 1965.

1. Mary's Earlier Record

When Mary arrived in Scotland in August 1561 to begin her six years of personal rule, she was not yet nineteen and had spent thirteen years in France. It is unlikely that the first five and a half years of her life, before she went to France in July 1548, had done anything to shape her outlook or character. It had been a troubled time for Scotland, with three successive English invasions, in 1544, 1545 and 1547, and a contest for power between pro-English and pro-French factions, but the child-queen had been sheltered from danger and the circumstances of her upbringing were not affected in any way which can have influenced her infant mind.

In France she had been the prospective bride of the heir to the throne for ten years, Dauphiness from her marriage in April 1558 until her husband became King as Francis II in July 1559, Queen of France for eighteen months and a widow after 5 December 1560. The character of the French monarchy, and the life of the French court in which Mary grew up, had been shaped to some extent by Francis I, an ambitious warrior and also a patron of scholars, poets, painters, sculptors and architects. But Francis had died in 1547, and the France Mary knew for twelve years was that of his son, Henry II. Henry inherited from his father the secular struggle of France against the house of Hapsburg, represented by the Emperor Charles V until his abdication in 1556 and then by his son, Philip II of Spain, who was the husband of Mary Tudor and thus brought England into the contest. Warfare was almost incessant until the treaty of Cateau-Cambrésis in April 1559. Against Spain the French arms had little success, and for a time, after a defeat at St Quentin in 1557, Paris itself was threatened with attack; but against England the French were more fortunate, and in January 1558 they won a resounding success by driving the English from Calais, their last foothold in France. This meant a measure of glory, but the cost to France of the long wars was national bankruptcy. Under Henry II, the splendour and extravagance of the court and the patronage of the arts continued, but Henry was not notable for either force of character or intellectual ability. Influence over this monarch lay with his mistress, Diane de Poitiers, and effective power was something to be competed for by the leading noble families, though their rivalry was to some extent kept in check by the mere existence of an adult king. It was after Henry's death that the reigns of his young sons were to give greater opportunities to the nobles.

Of one of the leading families, that of Guise, Queen Mary was a member through her mother, and her life in France is to be seen in a Guise context. Mary of Guise-Lorraine, the second wife of James V of Scotland, was a daughter of Claude, Duke of Guise, who had been raised to eminence by Francis I and who died in 1550, and she was a sister of the six Guise brothers who gained ascendancy in France in the later years of Henry II. The head of the house was Francis, Duke of Guise; then came Charles, Cardinal of Lorraine, who was Archbishop of Rheims, Bishop of Metz and Verdun and commendator of eleven abbeys; the others were Claude, Duke of Aumale, Louis, Cardinal of Guise, René, Marquis of Elboeuf, and Francis, Grand Prior of the Order of St John. Though not in the succession to the French throne, the Guise family could claim descent from Charlemagne, but they owed more to their ability and personality than to their lineage. It had added to the prestige of the house that the Duke of Guise was the leader of the army which captured Calais. Three months after that event, Mary Stewart, the daughter of Mary of Guise, had married the eldest son of Henry II. This seemed to assure the future of the House of Guise in the contest for power in France. But they were challenged by two other families – that of Bourbon, which stood next in the succession after the reigning house of Valois, and that of Montmorency, which was led by the Constable of France until his death in 1567.

Thus one lesson Mary learned in France was the meaning of a contest for power among great families. But the family rivalries were intermingled with religious differences, and the second important feature of French life with which Mary must have become familiar, was, in fact, the impact made by the Reformation. Ecclesiastical disaffection of one kind or another had existed in some strength even in Francis I's reign, but more recently the situation in France had been shaped largely by the proximity of Calvin's Geneva, which was a kind of power-house of revolt against both the institutions and the dogmas of the Catholic Church and which supplied dozens of pastors for French congregations. Calvinism won many recruits in France among the members of the legal profession and the bourgeoisie and also, as the years passed, among the gentry and nobility. Before Mary left France in 1561, the Huguenots were holding services in public in many places, they were taking over some of the parish churches and evidently had in all over 2,000 congregations, with, it was claimed, 300,000 members. In their great stronghold of Orleans some 5,000–6,000 persons were attending Protestant communion services. The first national synod of the reformed church in France had been held in May 1559 and, although it was a small and clandestine affair, it led to the adoption of a formal organisation to bind the congregation together.

Of the three leading families, that of Bourbon, headed by the vacillating Antoine, King of Navarre, and his more resolute younger brother, Louis, Prince of Condé, adopted the Huguenot cause, and, while the Constable Montmorency remained on the conservative side, his three nephews were Huguenots, and one of them was Gaspard de Coligny, the Admiral of France. The Guise family stood by the Church and were to become renowned for their bigoted ruthlessness in defending their faith. It should, however, be said that at this stage the Cardinal of Lorraine, an ecclesiastic of international standing and the statesman of the Guise family, was not wholly intransigent, for he favoured Communion in Both Kinds and he thought well of the English Prayer Book. There were many executions of Huguenots, and it was inevitable that the Guises, in power while Mary was the Queen of Francis II, should be a target for Huguenot attacks. In March 1560 there was a conspiracy, designed as a palace revolution with the object of displacing the Guises from their position about the King and of killing them if they resisted. The execution of the plot was committed to Godfrey de la Renaudie, while Condé, the real leader, was to arrive after it had been carried out. The conspirators were frustrated, and the Guises took a bloody vengeance in the 'massacre of Amboise'. Condé was able to deny complicity.

With the death of Francis II, the Guises fell from power, for the regency on behalf of the ten-year-old Charles IX went to Catharine de' Medici, the Queen Mother, who had been opposed to the Guises but had had little opportunity to resist them while Francis lived. The daughter of a house of merchant-princes, niece of Pope Clement VII and a kinswoman of many French noble families, Catharine had at one time been proposed as a bride for King James V of Scotland, Mary's father, but she lacked the royal birth which might have been expected in a wife of a King of

France; when she married Henry, his elder brother was alive and he was not expected to become king. During Henry's lifetime she had to take second place to his mistress and, although she continued Francis I's patronage of the arts, she had no political influence. After the accession of Charles IX, however, she was the effective ruler of France for many years. Her antagonism to the Guise family would of itself have made her incline to a moderate policy in religion, but she was also by temperament disposed to conciliation. In September 1561 there took place, on her initiative, the Colloquy of Poissy, which she hoped would reconcile Protestants and Catholics. It was a failure, but the fact that it had been held encouraged the Huguenots. In January 1562 the government conceded a measure of toleration or licensed coexistence to the Huguenots, as the only practicable solution of the ecclesiastical problem, and Catharine even prevailed on the Pope to give a degree of approval to this. The Guise faction were so hostile to Catharine's policy that they now left the court, and in the next year the Duke of Guise was murdered by a Huguenot. Wars, feuds and conspiracies continued.

The France which Mary Stewart left in August 1561 was assuredly no model of stability. There is no reason to believe that she had taken a keen interest in current affairs, still less played a part in them, but there were certain things of which she must have become aware. She had seen the strength of a reformed church organisation, she had seen bigotry on both sides, but she had also seen the efforts of those who were prepared to compromise. She had seen how religion and politics and ambition were involved in the strife of faction. She was familiar with a prelate – the Cardinal of Lorraine – who was also a dynastic statesman, she was acquainted with the subtlety of a politician like Condé. She had seen a battle, murder and sudden death. All these things she was to see again in Scotland, and her political inexperience when she left France in her nineteenth year, her innocence of the ways of self-seeking and brutal men, can be exaggerated. It has often been observed that she was initiated into duplicity at the time of her marriage, because, while the integrity of the Scottish realm was publicly safeguarded, Mary entered into secret agreements whereby she made it over to France.

So far as her private life is concerned, she had been married when she was fifteen and knew, or ought to have known, that the utmost propriety was expected of the wife of a prince: there is nothing to suggest that the example set by Henry II in his relations with his mistress infected the ladies of his family with moral laxity.

16

But Mary had seen, too, that the marriages of princesses were commonly dictated by political expediency. The one trace of a romance in her early life – unless her undoubted affection for her husband can be counted as such – was a kind of boy-and-girl attachment between her and one of her Scottish subjects, James Hamilton, conveniently known as 'Young Arran'. He was the son of Mary's heir presumptive, James, Earl of Arran and Duke of Châtelherault, and he was in France as, in effect, a hostage for his father's good behaviour. He was some four years older than Mary, and there seems to have been an understanding between them that, should Mary's expectations with the Dauphin not be realised, Young Arran would be an acceptable alternative. But Arran had been his family's candidate for Mary's hand from her infancy, and, whatever else may have been involved in this youthful attachment, even it had its political element.

It is very likely that Mary never received any systematic tuition in the art of governing Scotland, for it was not foreseen that she would return from France to rule that country. As Dauphiness and later as Queen of France, her prospects were of a life in France, and had Francis II lived she might never have set foot in Scotland again. She was more interested in her prospects in a third kingdom – England. Mary's grandfather, James IV, had married Margaret Tudor, elder daughter of Henry VII, and in consequence she was next in succession to the English throne after the children of Henry VIII – Edward VI, Mary and Elizabeth. Not only so, but as Henry VIII had married Elizabeth's mother, Anne Boleyn, while his previous wife, Catharine of Aragon, was still alive, up-holders of traditional matrimonial law argued that Elizabeth was illegitimate and that Mary Stewart was the lawful heir of Mary Tudor. On the latter's death, in November 1558, Mary and Francis actually assumed the arms and style of sovereigns of England. Mary's claim to England made a special appeal to Roman Catholics in England and to the papalist powers on the continent. France, which already regarded Scotland as a dependency, now saw it as a base for an attack to assert Mary's rights in England.

However, Elizabeth's accession was soon followed by events in Scotland which enabled England to turn the tables on the French. Opposition on ecclesiastical issues had been reinforced by patriotic resentment against the French-dominated administration of the Queen Mother, Mary of Guise, and in 1560 a revolution had taken place. English troops had intervened to aid the Scots against the French army of occupation, and by the Treaty of Edinburgh (July 1560), made between representatives of France and England, it was agreed that the French forces should leave Scotland and that Mary should cease for the future to use the arms and style of Queen of England.

Mary's prospects in France were extinguished by the death of Francis on 5 December 1560, and her expectations of ruling in England were, if not extinguished, at any rate deferred indefinitely – though perhaps by the acquiescence of most Englishmen in the rule of Elizabeth rather than by the Treaty of Edinburgh. It was therefore in Scotland alone that Mary was effectively Queen and exercised sovereignty, from 1561 until 1567. On her return, in August 1561, she found that the reformed church, while perhaps not enjoying much wider support than it did in France, had gained a degree of success which had so far eluded the Huguenots. The death of Mary of Guise in June 1560 and the withdrawal of the French troops in the following month had left the Protestants in control, and in August a meeting of the estates abolished papal authority and forbade the celebration of the Latin mass. On the other hand, the Roman Catholics had put up a poor fight and were temporarily demoralised in a way they never were in France. The country which Mary came to rule in 1561 was therefore one which had decisively rejected France and what France stood for and which was controlled by the reforming and anti-French faction.

The economy and society of Scotland were still fundamentally rural and feudal, and the smaller landholders and the burgesses were alike apt to depend on the great landed families, with whom political power lay. In the recent revolution, while numbers of lairds and many of the burgesses had given notable support, the lead had been taken by a coalition of magnates. By the time Mary returned, this coalition, formed to face a political and ecclesiastical crisis, was disintegrating, and there were therefore three or four groups on any of whom Mary might choose to rely.

The figurehead of the revolt had been James Hamilton, Earl of Arran and Duke of Châtelherault, Mary's heir presumptive. He was himself the most irresolute and ineffective of men, but the Hamilton family never lost sight of its claims to the succession, it commanded a powerful following through its many cadet branches and its numerous vassals and dependents, and it possessed a shrewd politician in John Hamilton, the Duke's half-brother, who was Archbishop of St Andrews. The Duke himself hardly counted once the revolt had achieved its ends, and the Hamilton interest was at this stage divided. The Archbishop – the Scottish equivalent of the Cardinal of Lorraine – was a moderate conservative in religion, but the Duke's son and heir, 'Young Arran', was now associated with the extreme Protestant wing, and had hopes, based on the youthful promises made in France, that the widowed Mary would marry him and would, as his bride, accept the reformed church. The extreme Protestants had the advantage of the support of some of the Protestant preachers, who had much influence through their pulpits, and in particular of John Knox, who, though he did not speak for all the reformers, had never any hesitation in speaking.

While Châtelherault had been the figurehead of the revolt, the most effective politician on the revolutionary side had probably been Lord James Stewart, afterwards Earl of Moray, a man who in his opinions and in his deviousness looks like a Scottish parallel to Condé. As the eldest surviving bastard of James V, and Mary's half-brother, he had unique opportunities of using his very considerable ability. While there is no reason to question the sincerity of his attachment to the reformed cause, he was too much the politician to follow the extreme line of Arran and Knox, and more ready to attempt an accommodation with a Queen who had come fresh from a country where Catholicism was more militant than it was in Scotland but where there was also some interest in compromise. In this moderate policy the Lord James was supported by William Maitland of Lethington, the subtle secretary of state, sometimes known as 'Mitchell Wylie', a Scotticisation of Machiavelli. Maitland was interested above all things in advancing Anglo-Scottish co-operation with a view to the ultimate peaceful union of the two kingdoms, and he was therefore anxious that Mary and Elizabeth should come to terms.

In the crisis of 1559–60, active native opposition to the revolutionary cause had been slight and the fighting had been mostly between French and English. Moreover, when the reformers' programme came before parliament in August 1560 only three or four peers had voted against it, while not even among the bishops who were present was there one prepared to take a firm stand. The most convinced papalist on the episcopal bench, Archbishop James Beaton of Glasgow, who should have rallied the conservatives, had gone off to France, never to return, and other intransigent Romanists followed him. Nevertheless, there remained a good deal of sincere, if inert, attachment to the old ways and of latent hostility to the new. It would be quite inaccurate to say that an effective Roman Catholic party existed at the time of Mary's return, but undoubtedly a leader with the necessary zeal and ability could have formed one. Typical of the situation was the Earl of Huntly, a magnate who was all-powerful in the north-east and much of the north. He had supported the revolution, possibly with some reservations, but he was a conservative by temperament and aloof from the moderate as well as the extreme Protestants. He, and others, could have been made into the core of a Roman Catholic party.

The provisional government which controlled Scotland after the success of the revolution in the summer of 1560 was still in power when, with the death of Francis, it became apparent that Mary was likely to return. There was evidently a sharp divergence between the extremists and the moderates, but it was the Lord James who was selected to visit Mary in France and instruct her in the Scottish situation. No doubt he was a skilful advocate of his own party, but Mary's own political intelligence may well have indicated the wisdom of following a middle course rather than attempting to rally the dispirited Catholics or capitulating to the more militant Protestants. When she returned, it was on the moderate or more politically-minded reformers that she relied, and Lord James and Maitland were her chief counsellors.

Although Mary never ratified the acts of 1560 in favour of the reformed church, she approved of measures which implied its official recognition, if not its actual establishment. Immediately on her return, and again on later occasions, she issued a proclamation forbidding any alteration in the state of religion which she had found on her arrival in the country, and in virtue of this proclamation priests who celebrated mass were from time to time prosecuted. A temporary solution of the problem of ecclesiastical endowment was found in an ingenious scheme which left two-thirds of the church's wealth in the hands of the existing holders – many of them laymen – and appropriated one-third to the crown, partly for its own needs and partly to support the ministers of the reformed church. Later an act of parliament gave the ministers the right to occupy the manses and glebes which by law and custom had pertained to the parish priests. This all represented considerable statesmanship, and, while it did not satisfy the extremists, who saw 'two-thirds freely given to the devil, while the third must be divided between God and the devil', it was satisfactory enough to moderate men.

On the other hand, Mary insisted that she herself and her household should have freedom of worship, and mass was said in her chapel, to the scandal of bigots like Young Arran and Knox but with the approval of many fair-minded Protestants, including Lord James, who sensibly remarked of her proposed mass, 'To have it secretly in her chamber, who can stop her?' Mary was probably as sincere in her attachment to the mass as Lord James was in his attachment to the sermon, but if her policy of Protestantism for her subjects and Catholicism for herself was a calculated one, it represented the opportunism of a skilful politician. Along with the Queen's mass there have to be taken into account the fair words with which she periodically reassured the Pope and Catholic princes about her intentions, and the all-round picture is of one who wanted to be all things to all men and to lose the favour neither of moderate Roman Catholics nor moderate Protestants, whether on the continent, in England or in Scotland.

Within Scotland itself, Mary's policy can be characterised as an almost unqualified success. Apart from the appeal which it made to reason and a sense of equity, the Queen's personal charm helped to commend it. As Scotland had not known a sovereign of mature years since her father had died in 1542, it was an agreeable novelty for all Scots of less than middle age to have a monarch resident at Holyroodhouse, and the opportunity for a young woman – and an unmarried one at that – to exert her personal influence was great. The uncharitable could speak of 'some enchantment whereby men are bewitched'. For one reason or another, criticism of her policy dwindled with the passage of time, and Mary was able to bring about a degree of unity among the Scottish nobles which had not been known for more than a generation.

But to some extent the policy being pursued by Mary – or by Moray and Maitland in her name – was an experimental one. What effect was it going to have in other countries? What effect, in particular, was it going to have on Queen Elizabeth? The intention in Maitland's mind at least, if not in his Queen's, was that Mary's scrupulously fair conduct in Scotland would facilitate an accommodation between her and Elizabeth, and he worked for mutual recognition between the two – recognition by Mary of Elizabeth's right to the English crown as long as she lived, recognition by Elizabeth of Mary's right to succeed her. There were two obstacles. One was Elizabeth's unvarying determination to nominate neither Mary nor anyone else as her successor. The other was the question of Mary's marriage, for that she should remain a widow was unthinkable. Elizabeth was nine years her senior, and the longer Elizabeth remained unmarried the greater the likelihood that Mary would one day be Queen of England, but to obtain the English throne without heirs to continue the succession would be a barren triumph. Mary's hand was sought by many continental princes, and it was obvious that a marriage to Don Carlos, heir to the Spanish throne, might offer a chance of Spanish help to displace Elizabeth by force instead of waiting to succeed her in the course of nature. On the other hand, any such match would end the possibility of coming to terms with Elizabeth. When asked to suggest an alternative to Don Carlos as a husband for her 'sister queen', as she liked to style her, Elizabeth could do no better than nominate Robert Dudley, whom she presently created Earl of Leicester and with whom her own relations were believed to be not above reproach. But even agreement to this humiliating match would not, it appeared, necessarily carry with it recognition of Mary's claim to the English succession.

The negotiations for a marriage with Don Carlos came to an end when that young man's insanity could no longer be concealed; and Elizabeth announced that she would not name a successor until she herself had either married or had declared her intention never to marry. Mary thus acquired a new freedom of action, and in July 1565 she married her twenty-year-old cousin, Henry Stewart, Lord Darnley, son of the Earl of Lennox. Like Mary, Darnley was a grandson of Margaret Tudor, and his mother, Margaret Douglas, Countess of Lennox, stood next to Mary in the English succession; but Darnley, as a future candidate for the throne of England, had the advantage over Mary that he was essentially an Englishman, for his family, the Lennoxes, had been in exile in England for twenty years, and Darnley had been born in England. The Earl of Lennox returned to Scotland in September 1564 and Darnley followed him in February 1565, with a passport valid for three months. Contrary to what is usually stated, Darnley, far from being a practising Roman Catholic when he married Mary or for some time thereafter, had conformed to Anglicanism in England and worshipped as a Protestant in Scotland. But some thought him 'indifferent' in religion, and his mother had close affiliations with the English Roman Catholics, so that his attitude had some resemblance to the politic opportunism in religious matters which Mary herself followed. The marriage was something of a love-match, on Mary's side at least, but Darnley was vain and empty-headed and the marriage proved to be a personal disaster for the Queen. It was also a political disaster. Elizabeth, although she had permitted Darnley to go to Scotland, professed to be furious, and it was in truth hardly to her interest that two claims to her throne should be combined; the marriage ceremony was a Roman Catholic one – though Mary did not wait for the necessary papal dispensation and Darnley did not attend the nuptial mass – and therefore repugnant to the Scottish Protestants; and the Lennox family was the hereditary rival of the house of

Hamilton, which had once envisaged its own heir, and not the heir of Lennox, as Mary's consort. The Earl of Moray, whose policy of an accommodation with Elizabeth had collapsed, gained the support of some Protestant notables and of the Hamiltons to raise a somewhat aimless rebellion, which Mary suppressed with spirit and resolution in operations known as the Chaseabout Raid. Moray and his associates took refuge in England, whence he had received some encouragement.

From this point a combination of political and personal circumstances, stage after stage, produced a series of misfortunes which within less than two years brought Mary's reign to an end.

There was now a political and ecclesiastical situation which was hardly of Mary's making. Moray's rebellion had suggested that no amount of concession to the reformers was going to prevail on them to give their Queen wholehearted support, and indicated that she might benefit more from cultivating the favour of Roman Catholics at home and abroad. The reformed church, therefore, now received less favourable treatment and there was increased activity in negotiations with continental Roman Catholic agents. Equally, the alienation of some of Mary's previous counsellors by the Darnley marriage, and the change of policy in relation to England, meant new men as well as new measures, and Mary, almost perforce, had to depend to some extent on the advice of men of less than noble birth. The most conspicuous of her non-aristocratic familiars was David Rizzio, who had come to her court from Savoy as a musician but was promoted to certain secretarial duties and, as some thought, to too much political influence. It was also believed, apparently without foundation, that he was a Roman Catholic agent. Against him, therefore, concentrated not only the resentment of the nobility who thought that Mary was neglecting her natural councillors, but also the suspicions of the Protestants.

But Rizzio's position in the royal household had another aspect. It was rumoured that Mary's relations with him were not merely those of queen and servant, and it was even said that the child of which she became pregnant in September 1565 was his and not Darnley's. This scandal is barely credible, and the likelihood is that Mary went no further than the dictates of her natural kindness towards her dependants and a perfectly intelligible liking for the society of a congenial and entertaining companion. However, jealousy of Rizzio's intimacy with the Queen was a pretext, if not a motive, to bring Darnley into the forces gathering against Mary. It had not taken her long to see that Darnley was no fit mate for her, and certainly no suitable person on whom to confer the 'crown matrimonial', which would have meant that in the event of her death he would continue to reign as King. Darnley was therefore at one with the nobles in feeling neglected by the Queen, and both he and they saw Rizzio as the upstart who had supplanted them in Mary's favour. Darnley entered into a bond with the disaffected nobles whereby they were to support his claim to the crown matrimonial, Moray and his associates were to avoid the forfeiture of their estates, and Rizzio was to be eliminated.

The murder of Rizzio was carried out with needless brutality in or near the Queen's presence on 9 March 1566. It can hardly be doubted that the aim, besides killing the Italian, was to endanger also the lives of Mary and of the child of which she was six months pregnant. However, Mary not merely survived the experience, but skilfully used her charms to detach Darnley from his fellow-conspirators and with his help to escape from their power. The murderers found themselves denounced and forced to go into exile in England, while Mary, by a further stroke of statesmanship, pardoned the rebels of the previous year, including Moray, and brought them back to favour. The birth of her son, Prince James, on 19 June 1566, seemed on the face of it likely to reconcile her with her husband, to open the way to security for her and to offer prospects of a recovery of stability in the country.

There is nothing in Mary's record before 1566 to suggest that she had criminal or immoral tendencies. Her conduct of public affairs, with all its opportunism and self-interest, indicates on the whole not only intelligence but a detachment which a woman of passionate nature could hardly have shown. There was little to suggest strong emotion at all, and even the Darnley marriage, though to all appearances a matter of the heart rather than the head, may nevertheless have reflected political calculation, for in a sense it neutralised Mary's strongest rival for the English succession. Only one sour-minded contemporary, an Englishman called Thomas Jeney who wrote (but did not publish) a tract called *Maister Randolphes Phantasy*, saw 'lust' as the motive for the match with Darnley.

There had been, in 1561 and 1562, two episodes which deserve to be recalled because they may possibly throw a little light on subsequent events. The first of them brought together in a curious and mysterious way Mary's erstwhile suitor Young Arran and her future husband the Earl of Bothwell. There was a sudden alarm at the court in November 1561, apparently arising from a remark of Arran that it would be easy 'to take her out of the abbey' (i.e., the palace of Holyroodhouse), and in the following spring, after patching up a friendship with Bothwell, Arran accused the latter of suggesting that the Queen should be seized and carried off to the Hamilton stronghold of Dumbarton. Arran was clearly insane, and from this point was in fact confined as a lunatic, but Bothwell was held to be compromised and the affair was taken seriously enough to lead to the institution of a bodyguard to protect the Queen.

The second episode concerned the French poet Châtelard. Châtelard, a descendant of the Chevalier Bayard, had accompanied Mary from France in 1561 and came again to Scotland in November 1562. The censorious thought that Mary was unduly familiar with him, and John Knox went so far as to say that 'the Queen would lie upon Châtelard's shoulder, and sometimes privily she would steal a kiss of his neck'. Châtelard evidently thought he had sufficient encouragement from Mary to hide under her bed one night, only to be found by two grooms making their customary search. A couple of days later he intruded into Mary's chamber when only some of her ladies were there. After his first escapade Mary had forbidden him her presence; after the second he was executed.

The impression one forms from these incidents is that Mary was not as remote or secluded as might be thought, and that if she had been an accomplice she might quite conceivably have been accessible to a lover, but also that the possibility of seizing her by force was not one to be dismissed as wildly impracticable. It is a little odd that Bothwell, who was alleged to have entered into a plot to carry her off to Dumbarton in Arran's interest in 1562, did eventually carry her off to Dunbar in his own interest in 1567.

However, the solitary piece of serious scandal which had appeared before 1566 was the rather improbable one concerning Mary's relations with Rizzio. It was all very creditable to a young woman in a somewhat rude and assuredly loose-tongued society. Mary had kept her reputation rather better than the contemporary 'virgin queen' of England.

2. The Kirk o' Field Crime: Facts, Circumstantial Evidence and Conjecture

It would be vain – and perhaps unprofitable – to attempt to review the events of the later months of 1566 without using the hindsight which comes from the knowledge that Darnley was murdered early in the following year, in circumstances which have been a source of perplexity and speculation ever since. Darnley, who had fallen ill in Glasgow, was brought by Mary to Edinburgh at the end of January and lodged in a house on the outskirts of the town, in fact abutting on the town wall. Known as 'the Old Provost's Lodging', it stood at the south-east corner of a quadrangular range of buildings which had been the residential quarters of the clergy of the collegiate church of St Mary in the Fields. During Darnley's ten-day stay at Kirk o' Field, Mary twice spent the night in the room beneath his, and was expected to sleep there again on the night of the murder. About two o'clock on the morning of 10 February the building was demolished by an explosion. Two of Darnley's servants were found dead in the ruins, and one, Nelson, survived because he had been in a gallery which projected on to the town wall itself. The bodies of Darnley and his valet, William Taylor, were found in the garden, outside the wall, with no external signs of any injuries. Darnley was clad only in his night-shirt, his servant wore a cap and one slipper as well as his shirt, and beside the bodies lay a dressing-gown, a belt and dagger, a chair and an indeterminate article which may have been a quilt.

For 400 years men have sought to determine who was guilty of the murder and to explain exactly how it was committed. It is impossible to shake off the fascination of the mystery, and all the actions of Mary and her associates in the preceding months are inevitably examined by way of an investigation, in the classical manner of detective fiction, into motive and opportunity. A complication – not unknown in some of the ingenious inventions of modern crime novelists – is the question whether the crime which occurred was the crime which was planned: in fact, while it was

Darnley who was killed, there is room for speculation whether he, or at any rate he alone, was the intended victim, and whether the plot was aimed at the life of Mary.

The traditional view – it can hardly be called an explanation, for it ignores too many of the facts – is that the murder of Darnley was a crime of passion, arising from the triangle of Mary, Darnley and Bothwell. It is at least true that Mary's relations with her husband were one of the most important elements shaping the situation in which the crime was planned. It is barely conceivable that she can ever have forgiven Darnley for his share in the Rizzio affair, and their reconciliation after it, if it was ever genuine, had lasted so short a time that within six weeks there was a rumour that an envoy had been sent to Rome to sue for a divorce. It is quite evident that the royal pair seldom – some thought never – cohabited after the birth of Prince James on 19 June. According to one account, a French envoy who arrived in Scotland while Mary was at Alloa at the end of July reconciled her with Darnley to the extent that 'they were together two nights', but the evidence is inconclusive. Their relations were certainly less strained in succeeding weeks, for they were together on hunting expeditions in August and it seems that when Mary was at Holyrood in September and Darnley arrived there she lodged him overnight in her room. In October, when she was recovering from a serious illness at Jedburgh, Darnley arrived and did spend one night in the town, though not in the same house as Mary. It seems very unlikely that they ever slept together after September at latest, and it became a matter of common knowledge that Mary now found her husband repulsive. 'It cannot for modesty, nor with the honour of a queen, be reported what she said of him,' reported the Earl of Bedford.

Whether Mary's revulsion against Darnley was reinforced by a guilty passion for the thirty-year-old James Hepburn, Earl of Bothwell, remains debatable. It may be that her emotional nature underwent a change in 1566, and psychologists may speculate whether after her experience of maternity she was more moved by sexual passion than she had been before. If so, it would be understandable that she was captivated by Bothwell, a man with a wide experience of women and very likely a much more compelling, satisfying and understanding lover than either the sickly boy Francis or that lanky, brainless and selfish youth Darnley. Yet, while Bothwell was undoubtedly in high favour in the later months of 1566, it should be said that the head as well as the heart may have entered into this attachment as well as into Mary's earlier attachments, for it was one that had much to commend it politi-

27

cally. As Lord High Admiral, sheriff of Edinburgh and Haddington, bailie of Lauderdale, warden of the east, middle and west marches and master of the castles of Bothwell, Crichton, Hailes, Dunbar and Hermitage, Bothwell was probably the most important man in southern Scotland. He had, besides, been conspicuous for his unswerving loyalty to Mary's mother. He had been a turbulent subject in the earlier years of Mary's personal reign, and had more than once been compelled to leave the country, but the Queen had recalled him at the time of Moray's rebellion and he had come back to Scotland in September 1565. Mary had learned the value of Hepburn and his Borderers in the crisis after the Rizzio murder. Here was the strong man on whom she could rely.

On Bothwell's side, although he had been married to Lady Jean Gordon, sister of the Earl of Huntly, so recently as February 1566, it would have been in no way surprising if he had set his heart on a marriage, or at any rate an affair, with the Queen. One of the characteristics of his house was an hereditary capacity for what was euphemistically called 'kindness' to widowed queens, and since the death of James I in 1437 there had hardly been a royal relict whose name had not been linked with the Hepburn of her day. Queen Mary's own mother had been thought to have 'over great familiarity' with Earl James's father, and when the latter had produced a divorce with a view to marrying that queen-dowager, he had set an example to his more notorious son.

Events after the death of Darnley make the conclusion all but inescapable that Mary and Bothwell were committed to each other in his lifetime. On the other hand, the picturesque incidents which are supposed to demonstrate that Mary's infatuation went beyond the bounds of discretion, and of which much was to be made at Mary's first trial, were very laregly inventions, which will be examined in Chapter 6. Allegations that Mary and Bothwell were guilty of adultery before Darnley's death were not apparently made until after the murder, and there is no conclusive proof – though, as we shall see, there are good grounds for suspicion – that their relations were other than proper while Darnley lived.

Mary's repugnance to her husband might or might not of itself have stimulated some of her nobles and politicians, from no motive other than sincere loyalty to their Queen, to seek means to free her from a connection which was so plainly intolerable. But Darnley's whole behaviour, ever since he had returned to Scotland and had been elevated to a fortuitous kingship through his marriage, had been such as to win him much enmity on less disinterested grounds, and it is beyond doubt that there was a conspiracy against him to which the Earls of Moray, Argyll, Huntly and Bothwell, Secretary Lethington, Sir James Balfour of Pittendreich and probably others were parties. One of the men who were arrested and examined as accomplices of Bothwell in the murder of Darnley was explicit, in his confession, about a contract in which Huntly, Argyll, Lethington and Balfour had plotted with Bothwell for the destruction of Darnley. His recollection of its substance was 'forasmuch as it was thought expedient and most profitable for the commonwealth that such a young fool and proud tyrant should not reign nor bear rule over them, and for divers causes therefore they all had concluded that he should be put off, by one way or other'. This 'confession' may not in itself be very good evidence, but it finds some support elsewhere. An English observer remarked as early as May 1566 that 'Argyll and Moray . . . have such misliking of their King [Darnley] as never was more of man'.

Moray later admitted that he had signed a bond of some kind with Huntly, Argyll and Bothwell, in Edinburgh, at the beginning of October 1566. He said that this bond was 'devised in sign of our reconciliation', and it has been thought this must have meant either the reconciliation after Rizzio's murder, when Moray was received back into favour in March 1566, or the pacification which Mary brought about between Moray, Argyll and Bothwell in late April 1566. But there were other reconciliations which fit better with the date in Moray's mind, namely early October 1566. For one thing, there was a meeting in September 1566 at which, in the presence of Argyll and Moray, Mary reconciled Lethington with Bothwell. However, the reconciliation which Moray referred to may be connected with an incident referred to in the document known as the 'Declaration (or Protestation) of Huntly and Argyll'. According to this, on some undefined night Moray and Lethington roused Argyll from bed and suggested that in order to induce Mary to recall the Earl of Morton and the other Rizzio murderers it would be advisable to oblige her by ridding her of Darnley; Huntly and Bothwell were next brought in, and the proposal for this reconciliation was put before Mary.

It is evident, therefore, that on more than one occasion we find the association of the parties already mentioned as signatories of a bond or bonds – Argyll, Huntly, Bothwell and Lethington – with the addition of Moray. That there was in existence evidence which Moray and perhaps others among the Protestant lords later wanted to suppress is suggested by a remark of an English observer in November 1567: 'The writings which did comprehend the names and consents of the chiefs for murdering the King are turned to ashes, the same that concern the Queen's part kept to be shown.' It appears, too, that an incriminating document with the signatures of Morton, Lethington, Sir James Balfour and other notables was given by Bothwell to Mary before he parted from her in June 1567; it would subsequently be taken from her by her captors.

At any rate, the various accounts of a bond and of negotiations with Mary for the elimination of her husband are clearly connected with what is known as the Craigmillar Conference, when Mary did take part in a discussion of her husband's fate. At this meeting, the four earls – Moray, Argyll, Huntly and Bothwell – and Secretary Maitland made an offer that, if Mary would pardon the Rizzio murderers, a means would be found to bring about a divorce. Mary was prepared to agree, provided that the divorce should be lawful and provided that it did not prejudice her son's legitimacy. After further discussion, Lethington made this oft-quoted speech to the Queen: 'Madame, soucie [i.e., worry] you not: we are here of the principal of your grace's nobility and council, that shall find the means that your majesty shall be quit of him without prejudice of your son. And albeit that my Lord of Moray, here present, be little less scrupulous for a Protestant than your grace is for a Papist, I am assured he will look through his fingers thereto and will behold our doings, saying nothing to the same.' Mary answered, 'I will that you do nothing whereunto any spot may be laid to my honour or conscience, and therefore, I pray you rather let the matter be in the state it is, abiding till God of His goodness put remedy thereto, that ye, believing to do me service, may possibly turn to my hurt and displeasure.' 'Madame,' replied Maitland, 'Let us guide the matter amongst us, and your grace shall see nothing but good, and approved by parliament.'

The 'Declaration of Huntly and Argyll', which narrates the nocturnal palaverings of Moray, Lethington, Argyll, Huntly and Bothwell as well as the Craigmillar Conference, was drawn up about the end of 1568 by Mary, or at least by Bishop John Lesley on her behalf, and is therefore conclusive evidence that she was aware of schemes against her husband which might be sinister or criminal; and the fact that she expected Huntly and Argyll to sign the Declaration is equally conclusive that they had been parties to such schemes. The version the Declaration gives would no doubt be designed to minimise Mary's acquiescence in the more unscrupulous aspects of the proposals, and possibly to exaggerate Moray's complicity, but it can hardly be a substantial misrepresentation of what took place. There are, besides, other narratives which evidently relate to this 'conference'. One, on Mary's behalf, states that Moray and other nobles offered that, if she should grant a remission to those who had been banished for their part in the Rizzio murder, means would be found to bring about a divorce or to convict Darnley of treason or 'other ways to despatch him', but that she refused such a bargain. Bishop Lesley, Mary's defender, himself states that the lords offered to procure a divorce if she would pardon Morton, but she would not agree. On 18 January 1567, less than three weeks before Darnley's death, the Spanish ambassador in London wrote to his King: 'The displeasure of the Queen of Scotland with her husband is carried so far that she was approached by some who wanted to induce her to allow a plot to be formed against him, which she refused, but she nevertheless shows him no affection.'

A bond for the elimination of Darnley was no more out of character than the earlier bond for the murder of Rizzio, with the same general aim of removing from the Queen an influence which some thought detrimental to their interests. But direct and open violence against Darnley would rise awkward questions, for he was King and to encompass his death would be treason. It would be another matter if Mary and he were divorced: this would right away set Mary free, and it would also mean that the murder of Darnley thereafter, when he was no longer King, would not incur any exceptional risks. Pending a divorce, however, the kind of un-concealed and unashamed action which had sufficed for Rizzio could be ruled out, and if Darnley was to be killed some more subtle means had to be found.

If the bond and the Craigmillar Conference belong to October 1566, there may possibly have been something of a lull in the attempts to solve what may be called the Darnley problem in November and December, when the approach of the prince's baptism (which took place on 17 December) led to the assembling of foreign ambassadors in Scotland and it was desirable to keep the more squalid aspects of Scottish court life out of sight. How-ever, efforts to secure the pardon of the Rizzio murderers were continuing, and this was a matter which many saw as closely related to the future of Darnley. The exiles evidently had powerful friends outside Scotland as well as at home, for even agents of the King of France had been working on their behalf a little earlier. It is less surprising that a faction which comprised the militant wing of the pro-English party should be countenanced from Eng-land: when the Earl of Bedford came to Scotland to represent Elizabeth at the baptism he reported with evident satisfaction that

Moray, Bothwell. Atholl and others had been working for the pardon. It was suspected that Bothwell, at least, saw the restoration of the murderers as a step towards 'a mark of his own that he shot at', and there is no reason at all to believe that any of those who took up the cause of the exiles did so without ulterior motives.

The Rizzio murderers were in fact pardoned on 24 December. In view of the widespread efforts which had been made on their behalf, it might be going too far to conclude that Mary had at last agreed to concede the pardon in return for an undertaking to rid her of Darnley. But it cannot have been merely a coincidence that on the previous day Mary had restored the Archbishop of St Andrews to jurisdiction which would enable him to divorce her from Darnley – and also, for that matter, to divorce Bothwell from his wife.

There is other evidence which strongly suggests Mary's complicity in, or at least knowledge of, schemes against her husband. In October, the reformed church, which had been complaining, with reason, of inadequate finance ever since Mary's change of attitude towards it after the Darnley marriage, received an important concession by an ordinance that benefices worth less than 300 merks annually should in future go to ministers; and now, on 20 December, it received from the Queen a direct gift of £10,000 in money, with victual worth probably as much again. It is hard to interpret this as meaning anything else than that Mary was aware of the probability of a crisis in which the support of the church would be indispensable. Such a crisis could hardly arise merely from the death of Darnley, whom few could be expected to mourn; but it would arise if she were to marry Bothwell. It may be that a similar conclusion can be drawn from the disposition which Mary was now showing to come to terms with Elizabeth. An ambassador – Sir Robert Melville – left Edinburgh for London almost on the eve of the Kirk o' Field tragedy, but his despatch obviously represented a decision taken some time before and indeed expressed in a letter Mary wrote on 3 January; this also is quite likely to reflect Mary's knowledge, or fear, of an approaching crisis in which it would be to her benefit to stand well with Elizabeth.

At any rate, whatever the precise relationship of the pardon of the murderers to the schemes for a divorce or other action against Darnley, there is no doubt that the pardon itself, and the consequent return to the murderers to Scotland, added to the number of Darnley's active enemies several unscrupulous men who felt that he had betrayed them when he abandoned them after the murder. This in itself might well have been fatal to Darnley, and it is certain that some of the Rizzio murderers were involved in plots for his assassination. In the confession of the Earl of Morton, drawn up just before he was executed in 1581, when there can have been no motive to conceal the truth, he admitted his fore-knowledge of a plot for Darnley's murder, and, while denying that he personally had art or part in it, he implicated his kinsman and client Archibald Douglas. And Archibald himself, in a letter written to Mary in 1583, tells a story which in inherently probable and for the invention of which there could hardly be any motive. This relates that about 18 or 19 January 1567, when Morton was on his way back from England, Bothwell and Lethington met him at Whittingehame in East Lothian; the fact of the meeting is corroborated by a letter from Sir William Drury to Cecil on 23 January. According to Archibald Douglas, it seems that Both-well and Lethington asked Morton to collaborate with them in killing Darnley, but he refused to do so unless Mary gave him a warrant in writing. Archibald Douglas was sent to Mary to ask for such a warrant, but she refused to give it. The fact that Douglas had no scruples in mentioning this in a letter to Mary indicates his belief that she herself had been well aware that schemes for Darnley's elimination were afoot. Morton's admission of fore-knowledge suggests that he became acquainted with the bonds already made by Bothwell, Moray, Huntly and Argyll, if he did not indeed become an additional party to them.

All in all, it can have been no secret that Darnley's life was in danger, and the French envoy Du Croc, who left Scotland less than three weeks before the murder, had 'some suspicion of what after-wards happened' and 'was not ignorant of the Lord Darnley's death to draw nigh'. Darnley himself was not unaware of his peril and it was partly for that reason that he had gone from Stirling, after the prince's baptism, to Glasgow, the stronghold of the Lennox family, though it is plain that he was not necessarily safe even in Glasgow, for his father was attacked there.

Mary's own foreknowledge of schemes against her husband can be taken as established. But this is a very different thing from concluding that she was a party to the murder, or even that she had foreknowledge of the particular plot which actually led to his death. On the contrary, it is easier to account for her actions on the assumption that she was not implicated in the Kirk o' Field tragedy. On 20 January she wrote from Edinburgh to Archbishop Beaton in Paris, mentioning a report that Darnley was planning, in concert with some nobles, to crown the prince and govern in his name, and she wound up the letter by complaining of Darnley's suspicious attitude towards her and of the readiness of him and the Lennox faction to make trouble for her 'if their power were equivalent to their minds'. Yet on the same day as she had written this bitter letter, she left Edinburgh for Glasgow, where Darnley had fallen ill, and shortly afterward brought him to Edinburgh. It is true that the engineering of a murder plot in which the tracks of the murderers would be satisfactorily covered was a difficult operation, but it is hard to believe that nothing more unobtrusive could have been devised than to use Darnley's wife as a decoy to bring him to a lodging in Edinburgh which had been designed for his destruction. Some other explanation of Mary's action must be found. Her defenders have alleged that, despite all that had gone before, she was genuinely touched by his illness – even though it was probably syphilis – and decided to nurse him; they have pointed to the fact that it was after his attack of measles in April 1565 that her original attachment to him had become conspicuous. But such a change of heart is hard to credit. The speculative suggestion – though it can be nothing more – may be advanced that at this stage Mary was suddenly struck by the fear that she was pregnant; and there is some evidence that, if she was not pregnant at this time, she became pregnant shortly afterwards, for it was said in June that she was 'five months gone with child'. Now everyone knew that any child of Mary's could not have been fathered by Darnley, who had now been completely estranged from her for at least three months. Mary might well have concluded that she must at all costs resume marital relations with her husband, at least for a time. On this view, her purpose in bringing him to Edinburgh was not to encompass his death but to preserve his life from the dangers which she knew threatened it. The idea that her aims were purely political, or even that she was bringing him to a place easy of access for his enemies, is hard to reconcile with the fact that she went out of her way to play the part of a loving wife, visiting him daily, twice spending the night in the room below his, giving him a ring and promising to sleep with him as soon as his convalescence was completed – which it would have been on the day after he was killed.

The strongest argument for Mary's innocence of the actual murder is her complete breakdown after it. All the letters sent in her name for a considerable period after Darnley's death, save one on 16 February, are in Scots, not in the French she used for her own letters, and this suggests that she was not taking any personal part in business. On the advise of her council, she went to Seton on 16 February for health reasons, and played golf there, but evidently did not make a recovery. So late as 8 March, nearly a month after the crime, an English envoy had an audience in a darkened room in circumstances which strongly suggest that she was unfit to receive him and was impersonated by one of her ladies. Even on 29 March it was reported that 'she has been for the most part either melancholy or sickly ever since' the murder. This breakdown suggests something more than the effect of the death of a husband she did not love, or even of a danger which she herself had escaped, and tends to confirm the possibility that she had been planning to preserve Darnley's life and again live as his wife. Her collapse would be all the more complete if she reflected that at an earlier stage she herself had encouraged, or at least not discouraged, plots against her husband.

The account of the murder which was designed to incriminate Mary was contained in the Book of Articles, submitted by her accusers at Westminster in December 1568. This document will be critically examined in detail in Chapter 6, but it is necessary to introduce here its outline of the story of the actual murder in order to place that story in its context and show that, where it is not demonstrably false, it certainly tells only part of the truth. According to this account, the place of Darnley's residence in Edinburgh had been selected by Mary and Bothwell before he left Glasgow, and on his arrival in Edinburgh he was lodged in a building which from its situation and condition was no place of security. Mary spent two nights in the room beneath the King's, and she was expected to do so again on the night of the murder; but powder had been placed in her room, and on the fatal night she excused herself from remaining at Kirk o' Field because she suddenly remembered that she had promised to be present at a masque at Holyrood in honour of the wedding of one of her servants. She therefore left Darnley and returned to Holyrood, whence Bothwell, after conferring with her, went to Kirk o' Field to fire the powder and blow up the King's lodging.

There are many obvious objections to this simple tale. In the first place, far from Kirk o' Field having been selected as Darnley's lodging before he left Glasgow, it seems that Mary's original intention was that he should go to Craigmillar Castle, a few miles south of Edinburgh. One account has it that the destination was changed because Darnley himself 'had no will' to go to Craigmillar, but it is not quite certain that it was he who chose Kirk o' Field, though some reports say he did. It seems a little improbable that the choice would rest with him, though he may well have expressed a preference. But there was nothing suspicious in the choice – if it was in the end Mary's choice – of Kirk o' Field, for it lay on the edge of the country, in a high, open situation, and was much more suitable for an invalid than low-lying Holyrood.

Secondly, it has been argued cogently that powder stored in the Queen's room could not have caused the explosion which destroyed the house. While we do not know the precise manner in which Darnley met his death, we do know a good deal about the character of the destruction of the building in which he was lodged. There was no doubt about the exceptional nature of the explosion: 'great stones, of the length of ten foot and of breadth of four foot, were found blown from the house a far way'; 'the house where the late King's grace was lodged was in an instant blown in the air . . . with such a force and vehemency that of the whole lodging, walls and other, there is nothing left unruined, and crushed in dross to the very ground stone'. The immediate reaction among all who saw the destruction or heard of it was that it must have been caused by a mine. The despatch which was at once sent in Mary's name to Archbishop Beaton in Paris described the violent explosion and added that it 'appears to have been a mine'. Messages arriving in London on 14 February and in Paris on 23 and 27 February also spoke of a mine. It is especially noteworthy that the Earl of Moray, who was later to put forward the Book of Articles, said when he was in London in April that the house had been 'entirely undermined'. It had evidently not yet occurred to him or his friends that an allegation that the explosion was caused by powder placed in Mary's bedroom would have been more damaging to his sister.

There are other difficulties, too, in the way of accepting the tale given in the Book of Articles. If the sole aim was to destroy Darnley, and the powder was in fact stored in the room below his, why was there such a long delay before exploding it after Mary had left Kirk o' Field for Holyrood? If it needed Bothwell's own hand to fire the train, why did he spend a couple of hours or so chatting to the Queen at Holyrood before setting out for the scene of the crime? If the final act depended on his agents, why did they sit beside the powder, with the King above them, until 2 a.m.? The delay increased the risk of discovery, and it has been sensibly remarked that if they 'had had any sense, they would have lit the fuse and escaped long before: . . . there was no need to tarry'.

The well-authenticated accounts of a great explosion probably caused by a mine not only make it impossible to accept the Book of Articles. They have long roused questionings about the scope and intention of the whole affair. Darnley could surely have been disposed of by poison, and no more suspicions would have been aroused than those which almost conventionally surrounded the deathbeds of the illustrious in those days. It would seem that the most likely intention of those who planned a great explosion was not to kill one man, but to kill a number of people. This in the first place opens the possibility that not only Darnley, but also Mary and her suite, were the intended victims. Now, it is quite conceivable that Mary's death was indeed designed. Any cold-blooded assessment of the situation showed that her position had become much more perilous than it had been at the time of the Rizzio affair, when her life had been threatened before. The birth of the prince had in some ways not been to her advantage. For one thing, her own life no longer stood between the country and the possibility of a disputed succession. Besides, if the prince remained in Mary's hands, he was likely to be brought up as a Roman Catholic, and the prospect of a line of Popish sovereigns was alarming to the reformers. But factious nobles as well as militant Protestants could see possibilities of gaining real power if Mary were out of the way and they had possession of the prince's person and responsibility for his education and indoctrination. Finally, the murderers of Rizzio, the majority of them in exile until the end of 1566, included the most ruthless members of the Protestant party, who had not hesitated to endanger Mary's life before and to kill Rizzio as part of a scheme whereby they proposed to rule through Darnley as a puppet. Now the prince would be the puppet. In short, there were many who would have benefited if Mary, as well as Darnley, had perished: indeed from the point of view of almost everyone it might have seemed the best solution. Bothwell, it is assumed, wanted Mary to live, but a married man who had made his royal mistress pregnant might possibly have thought her death the easiest way out. However, while there were many who wanted Mary out of the way, it is more difficult to determine whether anyone can have wanted the wholesale destruction of the nobles who were in her entourage as she sat with Darnley at Kirk o' Field on the evening of 9 February. And, if these nobles were themselves in the plot, and intended to kill only Darnley, his wife and their personal retainers when they were left alone in the house for the night, it is expecting too much of the conspirators' nerves to believe that they spent the evening at ease knowing the presence of gunpowder in the vaults beneath them.

Contemporaries found no difficulty about seeing Mary, as well as Darnley, as an intended victim, and this idea, like that of the mine itself, was one of the immediate reactions to the news that the house had been blown up. The letter sent off immediately in Mary's name to Archbishop Beaton said, 'We assure ourselves it was dressed as well for us as for the King, for we lay the most part of all the last week in that same lodging, and were there accompanied by the most part of the lords that are in this town that same night at midnight, and of very chance tarried not all night, by reason of some masque in the abbey; but we believe it was not chance, but God that put it in our head.' This is not likely to have been merely an expression of a view which Mary personally, if she was guilty, would have liked to circulate, and the idea continued to be accepted as one explanation of the puzzle, as was reported to Cecil on 19 March.

However, the idea that the intention had been to kill Mary as well as Darnley has not commended itself much to recent writers, who have been much more concerned with the theory that the explosion was the result of a plot, to which Darnley was a party, against Mary. There is no doubt that Darnley had been making some attempt in recent months to pose as a champion of the papal cause, and there is evidence that he was writing to continental Roman Catholic powers complaining of his wife's religious indifference. It is also true that the theory that he was a party to a plot to blow up Mary at Kirk o' Field is an attractive one in so far as it solves some of the puzzling details. But it is not difficult to detect what seem to be insuperable difficulties in the view that a Darnley-Roman Catholic conspiracy was the whole story.

In the first place, it is hard to accept that Roman Catholics, whether on the continent or in Britain, can have been convinced that Darnley was likely to prove more effective than Mary as the agent of the Counter-Reformation. However ostentatious the devotion he was showing to the mass in the later months of 1566, his past ecclesiastical record was at best so equivocal that even the most optimistic of Papists could hardly have put faith in his professions. It is in fact difficult to find evidence that the continental powers which Darnley approached did much to encourage him, and the letters he wrote to the King of Spain after his breach with Mary do not even seem to have reached their destination.

Mary's record, by contrast to Darnley's, while it had assuredly been disappointing to the more zealous Roman Catholics between 1561 and 1565, had not latterly been such as to cause them to dismiss her altogether. Pius V, who succeeded Pius IV at the beginning of 1566, was an extremist who can have had little sympathy with a conciliatory or temporising policy, but there is no sign at all of anything like a breakdown in his relations with Mary. He wrote to her – no doubt a kind of routine letter – on 10 January 1566, just after his appointment, addressing her in laudatory terms and exhorting her, 'Therefore complete what you have commenced'. Later in the year Mary sent off Stephen Wilson to represent her at the giving of obedience to the new pontiff, and her instructions to him are illuminating as to her professions if not as to her serious policy: he was to assure everyone he encountered – the Spanish ambassador in London, her own ambassador in Paris and the Pope himself – of her 'constantcy towards the Catholic religion and the obedience of the apostolic see'; he was to intimate her willingness to receive a nuncio; and he was to explain that she intended to arrange for her son's baptism 'to be in the old manner'. No doubt, of course, Mary had protested her devotion before, and her professions had not meant much in practice. But it was a fact not to be ignored that on 17 December 1566, less than two months before Darnley met his end, she did succeed in staging a Roman Catholic baptism for her son. Nor is it to be forgotten in this context that six days after the baptism she formally restored John Hamilton, Archbishop of St Andrews and primate of Scotland, to his jurisdiction. Mary's actions would surely have been enough to counteract any impression Darnley may have been making by his talk. Besides, Mary was aware that Darnley had written to Philip, and she took care, through the Spanish ambassador in London, to repudiate her husband's accusations of lack of zeal.

We are not dependent on inference, for there is evidence of what contemporaries thought of Mary and Darnley. A report drawn up at Paris in August 1566 by the Bishop of Mondovi, who was nuncio-designate to Mary, supported her claim for a papal subsidy and emphasised that her difficulties arose not only from Elizabeth's attitude but from her troubles with her husband, 'an ambitious, inconstant youth', whose part in Rizzio's murder is recalled and between whom and his wife there is such distrust that 'report says they have not cohabited since the child's birth, to the King's displeasure'. The bishop added this sentence on Darnley: 'He continues still to go to Mass, but, on the other hand, maintains strict friendship and intercourse with the heretical rebels in order to preserve and increase his credit and authority.' The only thing Mondovi has to say in Darnley's favour as a possible agent is that he was sufficiently ruthless to sanction the slaughter of the leading Protestants, which Mary was too merciful to do. In October, the

French ambassador, Du Croc, sent news to Paris of Darnley's break with Mary and of his threat to go abroad, and made it evident where his own sympathies lay. Of Darnley he remarked that 'there is not one person in the kingdom, from the highest to the lowest, that regards him', whereas of Mary he said: 'I never saw her majesty so much beloved, esteemed and honoured.' Somewhat similarly, a report from Paris to Venice in November said this of Mary, who was then reported seriously ill at Jedburgh: 'A princess, personally the most beautiful in Europe, and of a most cultivated and candid disposition, is about to die; and although this misfortune is of itself greatly to be deplored, other evils greater and more general will follow, as it may now be said that the Catholic religion will become extinct in that kingdom, both because those who govern and have authority with the King are its open enemies and also because the King himself is disaffected towards it. The Queen leaves a son . . . and there can be no doubt but that he will rather resemble his father than his most virtuous and religious mother.' There is surely little enough evidence here that Roman Catholic zealots were pinning their hopes on Darnley.

One of the arguments which have been advanced in favour of the theory of a plot by Darnley is a remark of the English ambassador in Paris, on 5 April, that the 'origin' of the death of Darnley came from Paris. But this is altogether too cryptic, and does not make it clear whether the plot which was known in Paris and which resulted in Darnley's death was in fact a plot against him or a plot against Mary. There was other gossip in Paris: on 21 February the Venetian ambassador there had written that the assassination was believed to be the work of the heretics, who also aimed at killing the Queen and bringing up the prince in their religion. It was said in Dieppe that 'they of the religion [i.e., the Protestants] had done it'. Any assessment of the state of opinion in Paris must keep it in view that Paris was nearer to London than to either Rome or Madrid, and was as likely to represent English gossip as Spanish or papal gossip. It is true that Archbishop Beaton wrote from Paris to warn Mary of danger to herself, but what he had in mind was a double assassination of both Mary and Darnley, directed from England. It may also be significant that the rumour was readily received in Paris that Lennox as well as Darnley had been slain, this was a piece of red-hot news, in Paris as early as 19 February, and may reflect the possibility that at a first glance on a dark February morning Darnley's servant was mistaken for his father, but the mistake is most likely to have been accepted by those who knew of danger to Darnley rather than to Mary.

The situation in Scotland was, at best, so ambiguous, and the real intentions of both Mary and Darnley so uncertain, that it is hard to believe that, at a time when negotiations for a papal subsidy for Mary and for the reception of a nuncio in Scotland were in train, either the Pope or King Philip would enter seriously into a plot with Darnley. Besides, when we take into account the long, slow and uncertain lines of communication between Scotland and the papal and Spanish courts, the idea that anything like a conspiracy had taken shape in time to produce the explosion at Kirk o' Field is quite unacceptable. It is admitted that Darnley had correspondence abroad and that from time to time he contemplated leaving Scotland to seek countenance against Mary, either on the ground of sympathy with him as a husband denied his conjugal rights or on the ground of his willingness to act in the Roman Catholic interest. There is also a hint that he had some notion of making an attempt to assert his claim to the crown of England. But it is easier to see in his behaviour the indication that one idea after another flitted through his inconstant, shallow mind, than to detect any consistent scheme.

The possibility is not thereby ruled out that Darnley, without continental aid, engineered a plot for his wife's destruction. But there are difficulties in the way of accepting this, too. In the first place, no contemporary or near-contemporary seems to have suggested that Darnley's agents planted the powder which blew up the house, and it is hard to see why, if this was known or suspected, it should have been hushed up. Admittedly, it was not in the interest of Mary's enemies, whose position came to depend on keeping her under suspicion, to suggest that Darnley was in part responsible for his own death. But there seems to be no reason why Bothwell and Mary, on their side, should not have offered a defence by accusing Darnley if a Darnley plot had even been suspected. Besides, Morton's confession in 1581 is again significant here. In it he does not accuse Mary, so he was not concerned to maintain the suspicion of her complicity, and yet he did not attempt to exculpate himself or his kinsmen by making a charge against Darnley. If it was indeed a Darnley plot that led to the explosion at Kirk o' Field, it does seem odd that the idea did not occur to contemporaries and was discovered by historians only nearly four centuries later.

Secondly, Darnley was at Kirk o' Field for only ten days, convalescing from an illness. It is argued that he knew where he was going to be lodged, and had made his plans in advance, but, as has already been observed, it is very unlikely that he did know he was going to Kirk o' Field. When he arrived there, he evidently thought that his lodging would be in Hamilton House, a residence belonging to the Duke of Châtelherault, and he seemed to be surprised when he was taken to the Old Provost's House. It has been pointed out that he was not likely to expect to find quarters in a house belonging to his family's hereditary enemies, the Hamiltons, and it has therefore been suggested that his expectation of going to the Duke's house was a mere feint, to conceal the fact that he had already determined on the scene of his intended crime but this does seem an unduly subtle argument. If he had not made plans in advance, then the whole conspiracy must have been concocted *ab initio* in ten days, and it is hard to believe that he was able to arrange a large-scale gunpowder plot, in secret, from his sick-bed in that space of time. Even his knowledge that he was going to Edinburgh at all did not antedate his actual arrival there by many days. No one could have had a great deal of time to work it all out, but almost anyone else would have found it easier to do it than the invalid himself.

A further argument against the likelihood that Darnley headed a conspiracy is his well-known inability to keep a secret. One description of his character says that he 'was so facile as he could conceal no secret, although it might tend to his own weal'. The Earl of Morton, in his Confession, said of him, 'I knew him to be such a bairn that there was nothing told him but he would reveal it to her [Mary] again'. Finally, Darnley was not likely to find allies in any plot he contemplated, for his betrayal of his fellow-conspirators in the Rizzio affair was fresh in men's minds.

There is, it must surely be said, less cogent and direct evidence in favour of a gunpowder plot by Darnley than for any other theory. The only piece of contemporary corroboration of a Darnley plot is an oblique one. George Buchanan, in his *History*, said that most of Darnley's attendants had 'gone out of the way, as foreknowing the danger at hand'. Now, Buchanan's thesis was that the only plot was one by Mary and Bothwell against Darnley, but it is inconceivable that Darnley's attendants knew of such a plot and did not warn their master. The 'foreknowledge', if such there was, could have come only through a warning by Darnley himself. If there is anything at all in this remark of Buchanan's it would go a long way to destroy his whole case, but Buchanan's writings are so stuffed with inconsistencies, as well as plain lies, that little importance need be attached to this.

The strength of the theory of a plot by Darnley lies in the explanation it offers of some circumstantial details and of the fact that Darnley was killed outside the house. On the assumption that Darnley's agents had planted the powder and that he knew of its presence, it is not unreasonable to believe that he awoke to the smell of burning, perhaps from an accidental fire, and fled for his life, only to meet his death – though this postulates the coincidental presence of would-be assassins in the garden. Such a headlong flight does explain why Darnley was almost naked, while his servant, who was not aware of the need for such extreme haste, had tarried to bring some warmer clothing for his master. This possibility is easier to accept – granted the premise that Darnley was the gunpowder-conspirator – than the refined theory that Darnley himself actually lit the train and then let himself out of the house. This requires the belief that he expected Mary and her retinue to return from Holyrood later in the night and that when he saw the torches of a band of men – in reality intending assassins – he mistook them for Mary's company and fired the powder. This, it seems, amounted to leaving altogether too much to chance. If the fuse should prove reliable, it might well produce an explosion too soon, especially as there might easily be some unpredictable last-minute delay before Mary actually entered the house. If the train should not prove reliable – and one of the witnesses against Bothwell indicates that contemporaries had not great faith in their fuses – there might be no explosion at all but Darnley's whole machinations would be discovered. Assuming that Darnley did supervise the firing of the fuse, necessarily in the lower part of the house, it seems unlikely that he would then return upstairs to his bedroom and let himself out of the window, instead of leaving by one of the doors with which the house was amply supplied. Nor is it likely that he would depart unclothed of his own volition at 2 a.m. on a February morning. It is also necessary to explain why he left two of his servants to perish in the house, while – equally oddly – the one who survived was on the gallery by which Darnley is alleged to have left the building. The circumstances suggest an element of surprise and haste rather than a pre-arranged exit.

When the news first broke, there may well have been conflicting reports, one that Darnley had been killed 'on the spot' – that is, in the explosion – another that his body was found in the garden, but the general concurrence of nearly all circumstantial accounts is that he was found in the garden, without a mark on his body. This makes it surprising to read statements in contemporary official documents that he was blown up with the house. The records of the local parish church noted that he was 'blown up with powder';

the Register of the Privy Seal and the indictments of retainers of Bothwell who were executed for the crime say that the King was destroyed in his own lodging . . . where he was lying in his bed taking the night's rest', or 'slain and destroyed therein' when the 'lodging was raised and blown in the air'. Perhaps the oddest thing is that one of Bothwell's own men declared that some days after the crime the Earl asked him, 'What thought you when you saw him blown in the air?' The idea that Darnley was in fact blown up has recently been revived. It is true that he may have suffered internal injuries which were not apparent, and one witness, a valet of Mary, stated that one of Darnley's ribs was broken, though he put it down to the 'jump of the fall' and believed that Darnley had leaped from a window. Yet, however freakish the effects of gunpowder may be, it is hard to believe that the body could have failed to be visibly bruised at least, if he had been ejected from his bed, expelled through the walls or roof of the building and yet found with no debris around him. No one has credited him with the invention of a patent ejector-bed.

It is much easier to see the flaws in theories which have been advanced in the past than to find another which is any more satisfactory. The plain difficulty is to frame an hypothesis which explains all the facts and preferably one which does so without recourse to the long arm of coincidence in the shape of the presence on the scene of two, if not three, bands of murderers all working in complete independence. But while it is difficult it may not be impossible, if we start with the few ascertainable facts about what happened on that February night and about the men who were active in and around Kirk o' Field at the time.

A beginning may be made with Sir James Balfour of Pittendreich, variously characterised as 'blasphemous Balfour', 'the most corrupt man of his age', who 'served, deserted and profited by all parties', yet, for all that, a competent lawyer who was a judge of the Court of Session, later its President, and for a time Lord Clerk Register. Almost everyone, both at the time and since, has seen Balfour as having a hand in the execution, if not in the design, of a plot at Kirk o' Field. Not only were suspicions about him at once in circulation, but it was reported that one of his servants was secretly killed lest his disclousures might 'tend to the whole discovery of the King's death'. There was also a link between him and one Captain Cullen, who, after his capture in June 1567, was said to have revealed the truth; at that time Cullen was speedily released, but when he fell into Morton's hands in June 1571 (after being in Edinburgh Castle with Balfour) he was promptly executed. Balfour himself said later that Mary had asked him to undertake the slaughter of Darnley and that he had refused, but little importance need be attached to this protestation of innocence, which in any event is not irreconcilable with action by him on behalf of other enemies of Darnley. As Sir James's brother, Robert, had received a gift of the provostry of the Kirk o' Field so recently as 9 December 1566, no one had a better opportunity than Sir James of preparing the ground for a gunpowder plot or any other murder scheme. There is no difficulty about accepting that it was Balfour who suggested Kirk o' Field as Darnley's residence, though precisely who put his suggestion into effect remains uncertain. Besides, it was credibly reported that Balfour bought £60 worth of gunpowder shortly before Darnley's death, and this was certainly not the powder which Bothwell is said to have brought from Dunbar and placed in Mary's bedroom. It rather suggests Balfour's connection with a scheme for a massive explosion aimed, at least ostensibly, at Mary and her train, whether or not Darnley was also intended to be a victim.

However, if Balfour had the opportunity, we look in vain to him for a motive, for he was manifestly not working on his own account. He was an agent. It has been shown that he had associations with Darnley, and even that he was, for a long period, connected intermittently with popish plots. But Balfour was probably the last man in Scotland to do anything out of principle, religious or other. It seems on the whole much more likely that he would be acting on behalf of the men with whom he is known to have entered into bonds for the elimination of Darnley – Moray, Bothwell, Argyll, Huntly and Maitland. These associates of Balfour had motives in plenty, as has already been explained.

First among Balfour's presumed associates was the Earl of Moray. His record gave much ground for suspicion. It was he who had raised the rebellion after Mary married Darnley; he had approved the Rizzio murder, with its threat to Mary and her unborn child; he worked hand in glove with the English government, which was all along opposed to Darnley's position in Scotland; he undoubtedly craved political power. Contemporary suspicions, no doubt based more on a general impression of the situation in Scotland than on any consideration of actual evidence, did see Moray as a party to the plot against Darnley. An anonymous writer told Cecil that it was alleged by Archbishop Beaton that Moray was the author of the King's death. On 12 March the Bishop of Mondovi wrote from Paris that most people imputed the crime to the Earl of Moray. There was a report in Paris on

20 March that Moray was suspected above all. On 16 March, Mondovi, after hearing news from Scotland, suggested that Moray, desiring the succession, also aimed at murdering Bothwell, the Queen's trusty servant and an obvious obstacle to his schemes. The gossip in Paris has the additional significance that there was a tendency there to see the hand of England in Darnley's death, and, of course, Moray was the most likely participant in any English schemes at this point as he had been in the past. These were rumours in Paris, but on 13 March, Moray, still in Scotland, remarked in a letter to Cecil, 'I am touched myself'.

Moray was an adept at covering his tracks, and it is not surprising that there is nothing to demonstrate his connection with the actual crime. The fact that he left Edinburgh early on the day before Darnley was killed has always seemed suspicious – just as he had been ready to enter Edinburgh on the day after Rizzio had been murdered – though the reason he gave was good enough: his wife had had a miscarriage. He left Edinburgh again on 7 April and was out of Scotland two or three days later, on his way to France. Before leaving, he had made a will in which he nominated Mary as 'overswoman' of his testamentary dispositions in the interest of his daughter, which suggests that, whatever his own part, it had not yet occurred to him to accuse his sister of murder. Moreover, while he was in London, just after the middle of April, he refused to credit the report that Mary would marry Bothwell, 'considering the Queen's position and her great virtue'. His decision to go abroad at a time of approaching crisis on the whole suggests that he may have had a hand in what happened and did not want to be further involved. It is true that the outcome of the crisis was unpredictable, but the Protestant interest might well be able to make capital out of it and he could return, with apparently clean hands, to play his part at the appropriate moment. He came back only after Mary's overthrow, to accept the regency which his careful scheming may have done much to put into his hands. There is no doubt that, whatever may be said about motives, Moray was the chief beneficiary of the death of Darnley and of the events which followed it.

While Moray took care to be absent when the crime was committed, evidence that Huntly and Bothwell were at Kirk o' Field that night comes from the confession of the Earl of Morton, to whom Archibald Douglas had said that he 'was at the deed doing, and came to the Kirk o' Field yard with Bothwell and Huntly'. There is no additional light on Huntly's actions, though he was certainly a close associate of Bothwell, his brother-in-law. As to

Bothwell's direct and immediate part, the detailed evidence, such as it is, comes from the confessions of four of his retainers – John Hepburn of Bolton, John Hay, younger, of Tallo, William Powrie and George Dalgleish – who were afterwards executed for their complicity. According to Hay's account, the crime was originally planned for the previous evening but was deferred because 'all things were not in readiness therefor'; Powrie said, perhaps in explanation of the delay, that gunpowder was delivered to Bothwell's lodgings at Holyrood only earlier in the evening before the night of Darnley's death. Some of Bothwell's men conveyed the powder later that evening, in a trunk and a portmanteau, on horseback, from Holyrood to Kirk o' Field, buying six halfpenny candles on the way and borrowing a match from some soldiers. The intention had been to put the powder into a barrel, which was to be placed in the Queen's room, but it was found that the barrel was too big to go through the door and the powder was therefore carried in bags into the room, where it was emptied on to the floor. All this commotion was going on while Mary, Bothwell and a good many other notables, with their retainers, were with Darnley in the upper storey of the house and presumably passing and re-passing up and down the stairs. When all was ready, the story goes on, 'French Paris', one of Bothwell's men, reported to his master in Darnley's room, whereupon the Queen's party prepared to leave. According to one report, Mary remarked to Paris, fresh as he was from handling the gunpowder, 'Jesu, Paris, how begrimed you are,' but she did not pause to investigate her bedroom as she passed it on her way out, and returned to Holyrood, accompanied by Bothwell. Hepburn and Hay remained with the powder – and the candles – evidently for two or three hours. After midnight, Bothwell changed out of his fine clothes into a workaday suit and went back to Kirk o' Field, with Dalgleish, Powrie, Patrick Wilson and Paris, answering to sentries who challenged them that they were 'My Lord Bothwell's friends'. Bothwell and Paris went over the wall surrounding Kirk o' Field, leaving the others outside, and, although Hepburn and Hay assured the Earl that they had lit the train, he insisted on making sure for himself. He left the house again after half an hour, with Hay and Hepburn, and as they rejoined Dalgleish and Powrie outside the wall the explosion took place. On the way down to Holyrood his party again announced their identity to sentinels. The Earl had a drink and went quietly to bed, to be roused half an hour later with the news that 'The King's house is blown up, and I believe the King is slain', on which his comment was, 'Fy, treason'.

47

Huntly then joined him and they went to the Queen's quarters.

These accounts contain particulars which strain credulity unless we are to believe that Bothwell conducted his business in a singularly amateurish fashion and sought to draw public attention to what he was doing. There can be little doubt that the confessions were extorted to incriminate Bothwell and designed to provide some kind of reconstruction of events to accord with certain evidence which had come to light. The highly improbable story of the discarded barrel, for example, looks like an attempt to explain the existence of something which had been seen. Bothwell's own account refers to a barrel on the scene of the crime. He says that it was found and that he preserved it, 'having taken note of the mark on it', but does not say whose mark it was. The chances are that the barrel was meant to be found and meant to incriminate someone or other. The story of the placing of the powder in Mary's room, apart from the improbability of the detail, is irreconcilable with the magnitude of the explosion. If powder was placed there at all, it was meant to incriminate Mary and consequently was not put there by Bothwell. But, with all qualifications, it is hard to believe that these accounts of Bothwell's actions are complete invention. He and his men were at Kirk o' Field.

Of the two other signatories to the bond for Darnley's destruction, Argyll and Maitland of Lethington, it can be said that both were in Edinburgh at the time of the murder and that Argyll, at least, was probably in Mary's company when she went to Kirk o' Field, but nothing is known of their precise whereabouts when Darnley met his death.

In addition to the signatories to the bond, there were other participants in the crime, namely the henchmen of Morton and possibly other representatives of the Rizzio murderers. Morton himself, though he had been allowed to return from England, was apparently forbidden access to the court, and there is no reason to doubt his own statement in his confession that he had foreknowledge but had not 'art and part' in the crime. Archibald Douglas, however, his kinsman, was at Kirk o' Field, as he himself admitted to Morton. Besides, when Archibald's servant, Binning, was executed in 1581 he gave circumstantial details to the effect that Archibald lost a shoe on the occasion – a 'mule' or slipper, which he, like others that night, was wearing over his boots as an aid to stealthy movement. The presumption is that it was Archibald Douglas who was the actual murderer of Darnley in the garden, for the king's dying words were heard – 'Pity me, kinsmen, for the sake of Him who had pity on all the world' – and the

Douglases were related to him through his mother, Margaret Douglas. It should be said that the only theory which dispenses with the presence of murderers in the garden is one put forward in a report, which circulated from Paris, that Darnley, alarmed by the smell of powder from the train leading to the mine, rose from his bed and escaped before the explosion occurred, but was suffocated by the smoke. This is, of course, irreconcilable with the account of Darnley's last words, which can hardly have been invented.

Finally it is not inconceivable that the Hamiltons were involved. While their initial attitude to Mary after her return had been equivocal, they had opposed the Darnley match and had taken part in Moray's rebellion in 1565. As they owned a house only a few yards from Darnley's lodging, they had, perhaps, the next best opportunity after Sir James Balfour, and they had motives in plenty for the removal of Darnley, the heir of their rival house of Lennox. They were soon, moreover, to bring forward a plan to marry Mary to Lord John, the second son of Châtelherault and younger brother of 'Young Arran', Mary's unhappy suitor of earlier years, and very possibly this was already in their minds. The Archbishop of St Andrews, who probably directed Hamilton policy, was in Hamilton House when Darnley was at Kirk o' Field, and there is a tale about a light in the Archbishop's window which was extinguished when the explosion took place.

There would seem to be nothing at all improbable in a concerted plan of action by some or all of those various individuals and groups. One of Bothwell's retainers said that his master had indicated that the leading conspirators had each undertaken to provide two men to take a direct part in executing the plan, and this seems a likely enough procedure, with the various tasks perhaps determined by lot. Thus Bothwell may well have provided men to move powder (though not from Holyrood, and not in a barrel), but it is perhaps more likely that the real task of his pair was to fire the train. The powder is more likely to have been brought in by others, under the immediate direction of Balfour. If the powder was stored in an adjoining building and transferred through inter-communicating vaults shortly before the explosion, it would help to explain both the delay until 2 a.m. and the readiness of the nobles to risk their lives in Darnley's room earlier in the evening. The part of the Douglases was clearly to contribute men to the party which must have surrounded the house to ensure that Darnley did not escape, and it was they who happened to meet the fleeing King. Almost the only untendentious eye-witness accounts we have of anything which happened at Kirk o' Field that night come from two women who lived nearby and who stated that they had seen a dozen – one said eleven, the other thirteen – men leaving the building after the explosion. It looks as if they had seen a section of a composite party. The Earl of Moray, in the early days before he decided to pin the crime on his sister, said that over thirty or forty persons were involved in the proceedings.

The fact that there were several principals, each contributing his subordinate agents, may go a long way to explain why the truth has been so elusive. It would be tempting, in fact, to see distinct plotters who were not co-operating in a fully agreed scheme. On this view, the large scale of the explosion may in some minds have been a mere feint, explicable to suggest that Mary as well as Darnley was aimed at. But others may have actually intended to kill Mary, along perhaps with some of their fellow-conspirators, such as Bothwell and his ally Huntly. The chance to kill Mary of course vanished when she left Kirk o' Field for Holyrood, and the delay until 2 a.m. might be explained by discussions as to whether the explosion should still take place, though now with Darnley alone as the victim. On the general view that Darnley, at least, was an intended victim and not a conspirator, his flight was not prearranged: he may have been alarmed by movements in the house, perhaps by the sight of men surrounding it; he did not take time to warn his servants, but his valet, out of loyalty to his master, did tarry to bring a chair and a dressing-gown.

If some of the leading conspirators avoided direct participation in person, some of them may even have evaded their responsibility to participate by deputy. It is unnecessary to go so far as to postulate two or three distinct plots, each known to only a limited number of plotters, though this would, of course, suggest that no contemporary may have known the whole truth. But, without going so far as this, it may suffice to say that among the subordinates charged with the execution of the scheme there was none who knew in full the plans of his employers. Andrew Lang had a glimpse of this when he remarked, 'It is not certain that the miscreants who blew up the house themselves knew the whole details of the crime.' One of Bothwell's men said that he saw none besides his own group, 'nor knew of no other companies'. This may have been put into his mouth to lay the responsibility squarely on Bothwell. But the summary of his evidence added: 'He knows not but that he [Darnley] was blown in the air; for he was handled by no men's hands, as he saw; and if he was, it was with others and not with them.' This sentence has an air of truth about it. There are also some indications that the conspirators were not all of one mind. One correspondent of Cecil remarked, 'Were it not for Secretary Maitland and Bastiane, who was married that day, her grace [Mary] would not fail to have lain in the same house and been utterly destroyed.' Did Maitland disagree with some of the others to the extent of wishing to preserve the Queen? It is further suggestive of divided counsels, or of something going awry in the execution of the plot, that Sir James Balfour left shortly after the murder and when he came back secretly two months later 'for some fear he conceives, he keeps his house, especially in the night, with great watch and guard'.

However, whatever the truth, accusing fingers were very soon pointed at Bothwell, and at Mary as well. It is true that the charges may have been to some extent inspired by those who wanted to discredit her and who had perhaps designed the crime partly to that end, but Darnley's removal was so manifestly – as it appeared – to Mary's advantage that inference was easy and, on the other hand, few could be ready to rush in with indignant assertions of her innocence. Cartoons and placards alluding to the guilt of Mary and Bothwell began to appear in Edinburgh within less than a week after the murder, and such accusations were apparently accepted even by Roman Catholics and others who might have been expected to be favourably disposed to Mary. On 11 March Archbishop Beaton had heard that Mary was accused of being the 'motive principal of the whole, all done by her command'. He was writing to her, and characterised the accusations as false, but others were less charitably disposed. The Spanish ambassador in Paris reported that Mary had got rid of Darnley, though he added that otherwise Darnley would have killed her. Equally the Savoy ambassador, who had been in Scotland, had little doubt that Mary was an accessory to the murder.

The next reports, inevitably, were that Mary would marry Bothwell. On 29 March, Drury, at Berwick, reported the belief that this would happen. In Paris the report by this time went further – that Lady Bothwell had died of poison, to leave the way open for her husband's marriage to the Queen. On 13 April a placard in Edinburgh ran, 'There is none that professes Christ and His Evangel that can with upright conscience part Bothwell and his wife, albeit she prove him an abominable adulterer and worse, as he has murdered the husband of her he intends to marry, whose promise he had long before the murder'. By 3 May it was said by the English ambassadors in Paris that Mary had arranged the murder so that she might marry Bothwell. It is quite possible that Mary was not at this stage aware of Bothwell's part in the murder. If there is anything in the theory that she was aiming at preserving Darnley's life, and had Bothwell in her confidence in her task of bringing her husband to Edinburgh, as she surely would have, then he could not have disclosed to her his own completely contrary intentions. Yet if Mary was pregnant it was in Bothwell's interest to dispose of Darnley, for with Darnley's death the Queen would have no alternative but a shotgun marriage with Bothwell. The likelihood is that Bothwell never revealed to Mary his part in the death of Darnley until he was safely married to her.

The preoccupation of historians with the questions of Mary's complicity in the murder of her husband has been to some extent irrelevant. The action which was fatal to her reputation in the eyes of contemporaries and which cost her her throne was not the murder of Darnley but her subsequent marriage to Bothwell. If, of course, she knew she was pregnant before Darnley's death, then her only hope of escaping shame thereafter was an early marriage to the man whose child she was carrying. But even had this fact been notorious, it could only have aggravated the scandal of an intended match with a man who was almost universally suspected of murdering Darnley and who was, besides, already married. Some attempt was made to give a show of responsibility to the marriage. Bothwell was formally acquitted of the murder, though by a trial generally thought to be a travesty of justice; a considerable number of notables were in some way prevailed on by Bothwell to put their names to a bond urging the Queen to marry him; and, in an action widely thought to have been collusive, Bothwell seized Mary by force and carried her off to his castle of Dunbar. But only thereafter were steps taken to free Bothwell from his wife – a process by Lady Bothwell in the new secular court for divorce on the ground of her husband's adultery with a servant, and a process by Bothwell in the consistorial court of the Archbishop of St Andrews for a declaration of nullity of his marriage on grounds of consanguinity. While Mary's desperation may explain her part in all this, any defence is impossible. The great difficulty about believing that the supposed abduction was genuine is that after her marriage Mary had at least one opportunity to escape from Bothwell and did not take it: when he had at one stage to leave her in Borthwick Castle, the lords who had risen in arms against them asked her to assist them against him as her husband's murderer, but she refused and the lords then left her in Borthwick. She may not have said, as she was alleged to have done, that 'she cares not to lose France, England and her own country for him and shall go with him to the world's end in a white petticoat ere she leaves him', but she does not seem in later times to have been able to make up her mind whether or not she had been forced into the marriage; sometimes she told one story, sometimes another. Besides, Mary knew perfectly well that when Bothwell had married his previous wife a dispensation had been obtained for their consanguinity and that this dispensation was deliberately suppressed when the proceedings for nullity took place. Nor is it easy to see innocence in a woman who, before Bothwell was formally acquitted of the murder, gave him a gift of church vestments to enrich his wardrobe. She did this in Holy Week, the last week of March.

The resentment and revulsion against the Bothwell marriage were real enough, and a remarkable unity in opposition was briefly achieved. As early as 1 May, a fortnight before the marriage and a few days before the conclusion of the divorce proceedings, some nobles convened at Stirling and undertook to strive to defend the Queen and the prince. It may be that, as was soon reported, they had it in mind from the start to depose Mary and raise James to the throne, but it was Mary's own actions which had made such a course possible. When the confederate lords assembled in arms, with the avowed purpose of punishing the murderers of Darnley, preserving the person of the prince, and delivering the Queen from 'bondage and captivity', it was soon evident that Mary and Bothwell had little support on which serious resistance could have been organised. On 15 June, a month after the marriage, the somewhat half-hearted force mustered by the Queen and Bothwell confronted the enthusiastic army of the confederates at Carberry. It was evident that a battle would have been a foregone conclusion, and, after seeing Bothwell safely off the field, Mary surrendered, to be brought in disgrace into Edinburgh, where women of her capital greeted her with shouts, 'Burn the whore'.

Mary was sent off next day from Edinburgh to the security of the island castle of Lochleven, and there, on 24 July, she was constrained to abdicate in favour of her son and to nominate as Regent the absent Earl of Moray, whom failing the Earl of Morton. Moray returned on 11 August. He had an interview with his sister in which, with characteristic self-righteousness, he upbraided her 'like a ghostly father' and, by giving the impression that she was in grave danger of execution for her crime, obtained from her a voluntary confirmation of his nomination as Regent.

He assumed office on 22 August.

The coalition which had brought about Mary's downfall had been based on the proclaimed intentions of the confederate lords, which said nothing about imprisoning or deposing the Queen or crowning her son. Consequently, it almost at once dissolved, and it was a pathetically small number of earls and lords who turned up at Stirling for the coronation of King James. Besides, the Hamilton family had dynastic reasons for opposing both James's kingship and Moray's regency, and they found allies in two other leading magnates – the Earl of Argyll and the Earl of Huntly. Just how strong the opposition was to Moray's policy was demonstrated when Mary escaped from Lochleven on 2 May 1568. No less than nine earls, nine bishops, twelve commendators and eighteen lords pledged their support and within a very few days a force of some 5,000 or 6,000 men was raised. But the Queen's army was defeated at Langside near Glasgow on 13 May, and she fled through the south-west to the Solway coast, from which she crossed to England on 16 May.

NOTE ON THE CASKET LETTERS

It may be doubted if the time and energy devoted, over the generations, to the study of the Casket Letters has been entirely justified. There are indications in plenty that Mary's enemies were unscrupulous enough to produce false evidence against her if they chose; and, on the other hand, even if the letters were proved to be complete fabrications Mary's innocence would not thereby be demonstrated, for her guilt, not indeed of complicity in the Kirk o' Field crime, but as a party to schemes against her husband and as an adulteress, is not open to serious doubt. Consequently it has not been thought necessary to devote a great deal of space to this topic or to quote at length from the 'Letters', especially as the text has recently been presented afresh, with a searching examination, by Dr M. H. Armstrong Davison in *The Casket Letters* (Vision Press, 1965). In the absence of the original documents, no discussion of the letters can ever be conclusive. The case for their genuineness has not been abandoned, but the examination and re-examination which they had undergone on the whole incline one to the view that they were not indeed forged, but were manipulated.

The alleged contents of the Casket, as they were produced by the Earl of Moray at Westminster in December 1568, in support of his case against Mary, were as follows:

Eight letters from Mary to Bothwell, none of them dated, but all evidently belonging to various dates from 25 January to 23 April 1567. The most important of them is No. 11, 'the Long Glasgow Letter', bearing to have been written while Mary was with Darnley at Glasgow.

The so-called 'Sonnets', actually verses in twelve stanzas of varying length, running in all to 158 lines.

Two contracts for the marriage of Mary to Bothwell, one dated 5 April 1567, the other undated.

If the contents of the Casket were wholly genuine and if they are read in the sense in which Mary's accusers clearly intended them to be read, this in brief is the picture they present. Bothwell had ravished Mary before he won her heart, but already while her husband lived she was passionately and devotedly in love with and wanted so much as to be 'between yours arms, my dear life'. She was Bothwell's obedient agent: 'I remit myself wholly to your will, and send me word what I shall do, and whatever happen to me, I will obey you.' She arranged to bring Darnley from Glasgow to Craigmillar for his convalescence from his illness. In dealing with him at Glasgow she was playing a hypocritical part, regaining his affection so that he begged that they should be 'at bed and table together as husband and wife' and prevailing on him to come to Edinburgh only by promising that she would yield to his desires after he was 'purged', or declared free from infection. She admitted that she hated what she was doing, and reproached Bothwell with making her play the part of a traitor. Her real feelings towards Darnley are expressed thus: 'Cursed be this pocky fellow that troubleth me thus much . . . I thought I should have been killed with his breath.' Mary knew of a plan to dispose of Darnley by violence, for she wrote: 'Think also if you will not find some invention more secret by physic, for he is to take physic at Craigmillar.' Mary formally contracted herself in marriage to Bothwell on 5 April, before he was acquitted of the murder and before he was divorced. Finally, she was a party to the supposed abduction.

The Casket was later said to have been discovered on 20 June 1567 in the possession of George Dalgleish, a servant of Bothwell, who had removed it the previous day from the Castle of Edinburgh, and to have been opened in the presence of the Earls of Morton, Atholl, Mar and Glencairn, Lords Home, Sempill and Sanquhar, the Master of Graham, Secretary Maitland, the Comptroller and Archibald Douglas. However, our knowledge of the circumstances of the findings of the Casket really depends on a statement made by Morton alone and uncorroborated. It has been pointed out that although George Dalgleish himself was examined a few days later, he was apparently not asked to testify about the Casket and the evidence he gave says nothing of it. It is true that the whole drift of his examination related to the evidence directly surrounding Darnley's death, but it may be that, if the contents of the Casket had been as important as they were subsequently alleged to be, the opportunity would have been taken to obtain his testimony as to its discovery. Yet it seems hardly possible that the discovery of a Casket at or about the date stated was purely a later invention, for there are several references, from that point onwards, to the existence of papers incriminating Mary. The first report, at Berwick on 25 June, was merely that a box had been found containing 'practices' between Mary and France, but by 12 July the Spanish ambassador in London reported that the Queen's enemies could now prove her guilt of the murder by 'letters under her own hand'. On 25 July Throckmorton, the English envoy in Scotland, wrote that if the lords could not bring Mary to voluntary abdication, they would charge her with tyranny and with incontinence with Bothwell and others and with the murder of her husband, 'whereof they say they have proof of the testimony of her own handwriting'. On 31 July Moray, on his way back from the continent, saw the Spanish ambassador in London and told him that Mary's complicity in Darnley's murder was proved by a letter she had written to Bothwell 'containing more than three sheets of paper, written with her own hand and signed with her name'. He related that in this letter Mary said she would fetch Darnley from Glasgow, would stop at a house on the road and try to give him a 'draught', which failing she would put him in the house where the explosion was arranged. Such a letter was also described by Lennox, who likewise was in London at the time. This letter has a certain resemblance to Casket Letter II (the Long Glasgow letter), but does not entirely tally with it. Had such a letter existed it would not have been suppressed in favour of the much less direct Casket Letter II, and it seems likely that the document described by Moray and Lennox was a preliminary essay at a complete forgery which it was decided to supersede by a more subtle concoction which was partly genuine.

If the contents of the Casket had at once been seen to be as incriminating as they were later alleged to be, its discovery would surely have immediately made the lords take a stronger line against Mary. But this is what did not happen. There seems, instead, to have been a marked reluctance to condemn her formally, whatever was being said privately and unofficially, and talk of 'liberating' her from Bothwell continued. If there had been any idea that her marriage to Bothwell was welcome to her enemies because it further inculpated her, one would have expected them to be only too ready to carry their accusations further after the discovery of the Casket. But this did not happen. On the contrary, on 30 June – ten days after the discovery of the Casket – the lords, including Morton, issued a summons against Bothwell for Darnley's murder and for taking the Queen by force and compelling her to marry him. This is quite incompatible with belief in the contents of the Casket as they subsequently emerged. Even on 11 July the confederates repeated that the Queen had been forcibly carried off and imprisoned by Bothwell – yet the letters proving her complicity were later alleged to have been discovered on 20 June. Three days later again, Throckmorton, who had arrived in Edinburgh a day or two before, reported that 'they do not intend to touch her in surety of honour, for they speak of her with respect and reverence and affirm that . . . they will restore her to her estate'. And this, he observed, was in spite of the fact that public opinion was strongly against Mary, the people affirming that 'she has no more privilege to commit murder nor adultery than any other private person'.

Formal reliance on the Casket's contents to support the lords' case was deferred until December. At that time the privy council agreed that parliament should exonerate the lords for their action against Mary because 'by divers her privy letters written and subscribed with her own hand . . . she was art and part of the . . . murder of the King'. Parliament therefore declared that 'by divers her privy letters written wholly with her own hand . . . it is most certain that she was privy . . . to the fore-named murder'.

This narrative would of itself suggest that the original contents of the Casket had been modified or had been replaced by other papers. Davison writes: 'Soon after Mary's imprisonment, the lords discovered a box which belonged to the Queen and which contained some papers of no great importance. Later, when the question of a tribunal in England was raised, a decision was taken to put the incriminating letters into this box, and the story of its discovery and opening was concocted.' This, however, goes too far, both in describing the original contents as of no great importance and in placing the 'concoction' so late as after the question of a tribunal in England was raised – that is, not until the late summer of 1568. A certain amount of modification or manipulation of the letters, carried out in 1567, might, of course, have been followed by further work on them in the next year. The description of the letters given by the English commissioners when they first saw them unofficially at York includes a reference to one in which Mary was alleged to state that she had brought about a quarrel between Darnley and her half-brother Lord Robert. This letter was evidently withdrawn and never heard of again. Equally a warrant by Mary authorising her nobles to sign a bond urging her to marry Bothwell was produced at this point but likewise never produced again.

Davison says: 'no forger, desirous of proving a guilty liaison between the Queen and her lover, would have produced such lengthy, indefinite and inconclusive compositions. We are therefore forced to accept a solution of a combination of the letters of at least two persons, with a few rather small additions on the part of a forger.' While the letters are less indefinite and inconclusive than Davison here suggests, the case which he and others have made out for an amalgam of letters, some by Mary to Bothwell, some by Mary but not to Bothwell, some to Bothwell but not by Mary, is convincing. Some of the phraseology in the love passages in the letters and in the verses is perilously near nonsense if written by Mary, but makes good enough sense if written by another woman to Bothwell. One obvious candidate as the 'other woman' is Anna Throndsen, a Norwegian girl to whom Bothwell was betrothed, if not married, but whom he abandoned. The letters were not in her handwriting, which bears no resemblance to Mary's, but they could have been copied. On the other hand, it has been postulated that the 'other woman' was a Frenchwoman whom Bothwell brought to Scotland with him in March 1565 and whom he subsequently neglected.

When it came to counterfeiting handwriting, there was little difficulty, for there were probably accomplished forgers in plenty and Mary's hand was a commonplace italic singularly easy to counterfeit. Some have seen Mary Fleming, wife of Secretary Maitland, as a candidate, and her own handwriting is very like the Queen's. Andrew Lang saw Archibald Douglas as a possible forger.

3. The Enquiry: Behind the Scenes

How startling the situation was which Mary's arrival in England created cannot easily be realised in the twentieth century. For generations now, England has been almost habitually a refuge for sovereigns rejected by their own subjects, notably a succession of French monarchs in the nineteenth century – Louis XVIII, Charles X, Louis Philippe and Napoleon III. And at the present day the world is well stocked with exiled *de jure* kings. But the spectacle of a deposed and refugee crowned head was less familiar in the sixteenth century, and – despite England's own example, a hundred years back, in dispossessing first Henry VI and then Edward IV and chasing them out of the country – the rights of kings to their thrones were taken seriously in Tudor England. Besides, Mary's deposition had not been the outcome merely of political or dynastic strife, she was suspected, if not yet formally accused, of murdering her husband and she had entered into a marriage regarded as scandalous and even adulterous. It complicated the matter further that if Mary, the suspect, was a queen, the murdered Darnley had been a king and, although from 1327 to 1485 the English historical stage had been littered with royal corpses, some sanctity was believed to be attached to the persons of kings. Perhaps the circumstances have never been paralleled. Assuredly no precedent for dealing with them came to mind at the time, and the possible solutions were many.

The one possibility which could probably be ruled out was that Mary should return to Scotland as she had come. Her flight had been a matter of impulse rather than of calculation: she had fled from her kingdom in terror for her life – it was as simple as that. But calculation was not likely to induce her to return. She did say at one stage that if Elizabeth would not help her she would go back to Scotland 'in that same sober boat wherein she came', but this was mere rhetoric. She would not go back voluntarily unless she could obtain English assistance, or at any rate meditation, or unless a revolution in Scotland should oust Moray and bring another faction to power. If Mary received no countenance in England, and saw no likelihood of an immediate revolution in Scotland, her obvious course might seem to be to seek the French court, in the hope of obtaining help there, and her requests to be allowed to pass through England into France were a little more serious than her threat to return to Scotland. But her prospects in France were not in fact good. Her brother-in-law, Charles IX, was a feeble youth of eighteen, the country had little respite from civil war, and the government was largely controlled by the Queen Mother, Catharine de' Medici, who was no friend to Mary. Mary had once insulted her by describing her as 'the daughter of a merchant', and at this stage – not inappropriately for a merchant's daughter – Catharine seems to have been more interested in the fate of Mary's pearls than in her safety. Since Mary's abdication a year before, the attitude of the French government as between her and Moray had been equivocal, and there had recently been indications that France would recognise Moray. All in all, the professed English apprehensions about a French naval enterprise against England on Mary's behalf seem rather forced, and it may well be that Mary's talk of aid from France did not imply serious expectations but was chiefly designed to improve her bargaining position with the English.

Elizabeth on her side could hardly defy humanity by sending another woman back to probable execution as a criminal, and she could not readily acquiesce in even the deposition of a sister queen, for her own interests compelled her to defend the rights of *de jure* sovereigns. She had, as a matter of fact, denounced Mary's deposition in the previous year, she had never given formal recognition to Moray's government, and on hearing of Mary's escape from Lochleven she had sent a message of congratulation and an offer to mediate. Both her instinctive reaction when Mary arrived in England and the logic of her past attitude inclined her to support Mary's cause, and the risks inseparable from Mary's claim to the English throne do not at this stage seem to have influenced her. The outcome which actually materialised – Mary's detention in England without a fair trial – must have seemed at this stage all but inconceivable.

The dilemma posed for the English government by Mary's arrival can be seen through the eyes of Mr Secretary Cecil, an indefatigable writer of memoranda. Like other English councillors, Cecil was not affected either by the emotional appeal which Mary's plight made to his Queen or by abstract concepts of justice, and he coolly analysed circumstances and possible lines of policy. Within a few days of Mary's arrival in England he wrote the first of many papers in which he assessed the situation. He discerned difficulties and dangers in every possible course of action. He was quite clear that the English government could not simply decline to accept any responsibility, if only because Mary, besides being Elizabeth's heir by right of blood, had laid a claim to the crown of England 'not as second person after the Queen's Majesty, but before her'. He also resurrected the antiquated pretension that England's superiority over the crown of Scotland could be proved by 'multitude of records, examples and precedents'. Yet, while the secretary thought that his Queen must intervene, he could not see what course it was most politic to pursue. Among the dangers if Mary should 'pass to France' would be the revival of the Franco-Scottish alliance and perhaps French action in support of Mary's claim to England. Among the dangers if she remained in England would be the use of her claims to Elizabeth's throne to create a focus of disaffection. If she returned to Scotland, the friends of England there would be abased, those of France elevated, and there would be constant danger of war. Cecil was later to sum up the English dilemma more succinctly: we find, he said, 'neither her continuance here good, nor her departing hence quiet for us'.

At this stage, while Cecil did not see a clear way ahead, he was obviously already inclined to the idea of an investigation in which both Mary and her accusers should be heard and the opportunity taken to drive a bargain advantageous to England. He had always thought an alliance with Scotland 'profitable' to England, both in the interests of the Protestant religion and for security against France and other powers. Therefore, should Mary be tried and acquitted, she ought to be required, 'in consideration of the benefit' of acquittal, to ratify the Treaty of Edinburgh, with its renunciation of her claim to England. Should she be found guilty, she should either be restored under limitations, perhaps to share sovereignty with her son, or, 'if the criminality be excessive, to live in some convenient place without possessing her kingdom'. This was manifestly a weighted assessment. Cecil obviously did not much care whether Mary was guilty or innocent, for if she was innocent there was no case at all for exacting a price for her acquittal. It is difficult to avoid the conclusion that he was resolutely opposed to Mary's restoration, and he even argued that her restoration would not be in her own interest. He professed to believe that if she went back to Scotland as Queen 'the young prince shall have but a short time' and 'most likely the Queen herself shall not have long continuance', but it is a little difficult to square this prediction with his prophecy that her return would bring the friends of France to power, for Mary's enemies hitherto had been the friends of England, not those of France.

The one possibility that Cecil's survey did not take into account was that Mary might find another husband, and in this he was somewhat obtuse, for, whether in France, Scotland or England, this twenty-five-years-old queen, with only one infant son, was bound to be the focus of matrimonial ambitions and calculations.

The secretary could sum things up in the cool detachment of London. To be dispassionate was much harder for those who were in personal touch with the refugee Queen. Mary had arrived in England on the evening of 16 May, and a day or two after receiving the news Elizabeth instructed Sir Francis Knollys and Lord Scrope to interview her. Knollys, Elizabeth's vice-chamberlain, was married to a niece of Elizabeth's mother, and so had a special and privileged position in the English Queen's immediate circle. He was, however, deeply committed to the ultra-Protestant wing among the English reformers and openly critical of the Prayer Book which his Queen upheld. Scrope, the owner of Bolton Castle, had been governor of Carlisle and warden of the west marches since 1562. His wife was a sister of the Duke of Norfolk. Knollys and Scrope saw Mary on their arrival at Carlisle on 28 May, and in the discussion they had there can already be detected some of the elements which were to persist in all the investigations made into the charges against the Scottish Queen. Mary asked now, as she was to do all along, to be allowed to speak in Elizabeth's presence. Her defence was that the charges against her were a mere pretext, and she had counter-accusations to make. So far from the guilt of Darnley's death being hers, 'both Lethington and the Lord Morton were assenting to the murder of her husband, as it could well be proved, although now they would seem to pursue others for the same'. In reply, Scrope and Knollys cautiously informed Mary that she could not be 'solemnly and worthily' admitted to Elizabeth's presence 'by reason of the great slander of murder, of which she was not yet purged', but assured her that if she could prove her innocence she would have Elizabeth's support. When Mary retorted that the English Queen should at least give her a passage through England to France to seek continental aid, it was answered that if she gained help from Elizabeth she would not need to seek it abroad. In making this remark, Scrope and Knollys were, whether consciously or not, the spokesmen of a central point of English policy, which was to keep Mary's hopes of English help alive and therefore make her less likely to look elsewhere. Apart, however, from thus using the prospect of English aid to prevent her from looking to the continent, they warned her that Elizabeth could not look favourably on any attempt to enlist foreign assistance, the 'imminent danger' of which she 'could not suffer'. Yet, while the Englishmen firmly put an English viewpoint in their conversation with Mary, they felt obliged, when they made a report to their sovereign, to observe that she would be open to criticism if she detained Mary and that it was inconsistent with honour to keep her 'so rigorously as a prisoner'.

The puritanical Knollys, cousin of Elizabeth though he was, cannot have been predisposed to favour Mary, but there is no doubt that his attitude was much influenced by her personal appeal. At the first interview she had with the two Englishmen she had impressed them with her 'eloquent tongues and discreet head, stout courage and liberal heart'. Sometimes, indeed, she could be rather tiresome, when she 'fell into her ordinary inveighing against my Lord of Moray and his adherents' or when she revealed too bluntly her 'bloody appetite to shed the blood of her enemies'. On such occasions Knollys had to indicate to her that there might be another side to the story. He told her that princes might sometimes be deposed, for instance for lunacy, and asked plainly, 'What difference is there between lunacy and cruel murdering?' When so reproached, Mary began 'to clear herself after her accustomed manner' and 'the tears fell from her eyes'. Mary was always easily moved to 'tears in greater abundance than the matter required', as John Knox had put it, but the weeping which had left the reformer unmoved had its effect on the English courtier, who felt he had to comfort her with an assurance that Elizabeth 'would be the gladdest in the world to see her grace well purged of that crime', so that she 'might aid her fully and amply to the advancement of her grace to her government royal again'. Further interviews did not make things any easier for Knollys. Mary, he declared after one of them, was 'a notable woman', who showed a great desire for vengeance on her enemies by any means, but who also admired courage whether in friend or foe and to whom 'for victory's sake pain and peril seem pleasant'. After still more experience of the captive, he admitted that he 'must commend this Queen's policy, ready wit and constant courage', and he was so deeply moved as to exclaim to Cecil: 'What is to be done with such a lady and princess, or whether such a puissant lady be nourished in one's bosom, or whether it be good to halt and dissemble with such a lady, I refer to your judgement'. This was an implied criticism of the secretary, who did not have the embarrassment of dealing with Mary in person. But the letters from Knollys may well have brought home to Cecil that Mary must not be allowed to bring her charm into play at any investigation and must therefore be at all costs prevented from appearing in person.

The idea of some kind of enquiry or investigation appealed to all parties, though not for identical reasons. Cecil had seen at the outset that the English government might base its decision about Mary's future, at least ostensibly, on the findings of a judicial tribunal of some kind. It was, indeed, evident that in Cecil's view political considerations rather than justice would determine Mary's fate, but the prospect of an investigation could be made to look attractive. The idea was put before Mary, by implication at least, when Knollys, at his first interview with her on 28 May, had indicated that she must clear herself of the charges against her before she could expect Elizabeth's help. Mary evidently accepted the implication in a general way: whereas her first letter to Elizabeth after her arrival in England had been merely an appeal for pity on a helpless refugee, she now, on 28 May, wrote at greater length, complaining of her detention and offering to appear before Elizabeth to purge herself of the calumnies of her enemies, so that the English Queen would champion her 'just cause' until her restoration was effected. The second letter was conveyed to the English court by Lord Herries, who had accompanied Mary on her flight from Scotland, and was received on 5 June. On 8 June, Elizabeth sent a reply, by the hand of Henry Middlemore; he was a cousin of Sir Nicholas Throckmorton and had been in Scotland in the previous year to report on James's coronation. In the letter which Middlemore carried, Elizabeth reaffirmed that, whatever her regard for Mary, she would never be so careless of her own reputation as to receive Mary until she had first been acquitted. This meant, not a hearing by Elizabeth in person, which Mary wanted, but an enquiry by agents of the English government, and Cecil had instructed Middlemore to underline this by explaining the English attitude more fully. He was to give Mary an assurance that 'the Queen meaneth to take her and her cause into her protection, and according to the justice of her cause will prosecute all her adversaries'. But Elizabeth could not receive Mary as long as she was under suspicion of the horrible crimes of failing to avenge the death of Darnley, who was Elizabeth's near kinsman, and of marrying the murderer when he had been divorced for adultery by his lawful wife. The position, in brief, was that Elizabeth neither condemned nor acquitted Mary until she should have more information, and Middlemore was to say that she wanted Mary to be brought to some place nearer the court, where she could have more pleasure and liberty than she had at Carlisle. Middlemore arrived at Carlisle, with Elizabeth's letter and Cecil's instructions, on 12 June, and met Mary on the 13th. It was a very stormy interview, with 'much passion and weeping'. Mary raged for vengeance on her enemies and said that she would not move further into England unless she was going to see Elizabeth. She made a good point by observing that when Moray had been a fugitive from Scotland in 1565, after raising a rebellion against his lawful sovereign, he had been received by Elizabeth. Should she be detained in England against her will, her cause would be prosecuted by her lieutenant, the Duke of Châtelherault, with French aid. Middlemore could only repeat the substance of Elizabeth's message. Mary in return complained of her usage at Elizabeth's hands and said that she 'had no other judge but God: none could take upon them to judge of her: she knew her degree of estate well enough'. It was not going to be easy to bring Mary to submit to an enquiry.

The other party who would be chiefly concerned in any investigation – Moray and his faction – had taken the initiative in communicating with the English government and were ready to appear as Mary's accusers. After all, they had taken the responsibility of carrying through a revolution against their sovereign which had brought on them the suspicion, if not the hostility, of England: if they were now going to be challenged as a result of an appeal by Mary, their whole future depended on the effectiveness of the propaganda. On hearing that Mary had reached England, Moray had lost little time, and on 21 May he sent his secretary, John Wood, to the English court, where he would arrive about 26 or 27 May. Not only so, but, possibly prompted by a hint from Cecil about the prospect of an investigation, Moray soon set about preparing his case. It has been suggested that George Buchanan was almost at once instructed to start preparing an indictment of the fugitive Queen, in the shape of a first draft of his *Detection of Mary Queen of Scots*. The official response of the English government to Moray's approach through Wood came in a letter from Elizabeth to Moray, written on 8 June and, like her letter to Mary of the same date, entrusted to Middlemore, who proceeded north after his meeting with Mary at Carlisle. Elizabeth was not prepared to accept Moray in his self-appointed rôle of accuser of Mary: on the contrary, he must inform her of his defence against 'such weighty crimes and causes as the said

5

Queen has already or shall hereafter object against you'. The prospect thus being held out was one of a quasi-judicial investigation in which the representatives of the English Queen would hear accusations and counter-accusations between the two parties.

This was not what Moray had envisaged, and he was alarmed at the prospect of an investigation the outcome of which might be a decision by the English government to restore Mary. He had had previous experience of Elizabeth's unreliability, for in 1565 she had first secretly encouraged him to rebel against Mary after the Darnley marriage and then had publicly repudiated and denounced him when the rebellion failed. He could not, therefore, now risk accusing the woman who had been, and might again be, his lawful sovereign, unless he had some irrevocable guarantee for his future. Consequently, after he had received from Middlemore Elizabeth's letter of 8 June demanding that he must in effect justify his rebellion by countering Mary's charges, he wrote, on 28 June, to try to elicit from Elizabeth some such assurance: 'In case the Queen's Majesty will have the accusation directly to proceed, it were most reasonable we understood what we should look to follow thereupon in case we prove all that we allege. Otherwise we shall be as uncertain after the cause concluded as we are presently.' He mentioned that he had already sent to John Wood, at the English court, material which would 'resolve' Elizabeth's doubts, but he made it clear that he had further and more damning material, in the form of letters, which would be fatal to Mary if they were accepted as conclusive evidence but might be fatal to him if they were not. He asked that copies of the letters, which were in Wood's hands, 'may be considered by the judges that shall have the examination and commission of the matter, that they may resolve us this far, in case the principals agree with the copies, that then we prove the cause indeed'. This can be taken as tantamount to asking for a favourable verdict in advance, without regard to the readiness and ability of Mary's supporters to challenge his evidence, but it has also been suggested that the inference should be that if the existing material, as displayed in the copies, was not thought decisive, the 'principals' could be suitably amended.

There is no evidence that Moray received a reply at this stage. Cecil did draft notes on his questionings, on 30 June, and they would not have been very encouraging to Moray had they ever reached him. The points Cecil made were that Elizabeth never meant to have Mary accused, far less condemned, but aimed only at a reconciliation between her and her subjects, and that no 'proofs' should be taken as sufficient without the hearing of both parties. Yet, whether or not Moray received some assurance, and even although he could not look forward now to appearing in the first place as the prosecutor, he could hardly refuse to appear to answer Mary's accusations and so let his case go by default. And he could answer Mary's accusations only by counter-accusations. On 13 July, therefore, he agreed to take part in an enquiry. Writing to Elizabeth, he said that he had information from John Wood and that he would with all possible diligence either come in person or 'expede to her majesty' some others of credit and experience to 'prosecute this cause so far as she shall think expedient for her information'. When he learned what time and place were appointed, he would arrange to appear either in person or by delegates. On 22 July Elizabeth replied, saying that she had informed Lord Herries, Mary's representative, of Moray's willingness to appear 'to treat in that great matter concerning the Queen of Scots', but added that 'during the treating nothing would be done, or intended in any way', to the prejudice of Mary.

That last sentence was little comfort to Moray, but had Elizabeth not made some such statement it would have been impossible to prevail on Mary to submit to the investigation. Neither now nor later did Mary see herself as appearing in the capacity of an accused person before a tribunal with power to pass judgement upon her. Not only did she take her stand on her position as a sovereign princess, over whom no court had jurisdiction, but, although she was aware that evidence would certainly be produced against her, she conceived the investigation as a preliminary to her restoration. In her optimistic approach she was on the whole encouraged by Elizabeth. On 22 June her envoys, Lords Herries and Fleming, had an interview with Elizabeth and some of her councillors. Herries declared that if Elizabeth would neither aid Mary nor let her seek help elsewhere she would return to Scotland, that she would not answer accusations except in Elizabeth's presence and that she would not move to any other place in England without force unless she was going to see the English Queen. Elizabeth laid down as a condition of assistance that the charges against Mary must first be investigated by her, not, however, as a judge, but as Mary's friend, so that she could discover by what authority her enemies had deprived her of her crown. Elizabeth therefore wanted Mary to come to some place within fifty or sixty miles of London, where the enquiry might take place before certain councillors. She could not allow Mary to return to Scotland in her present 'sober equipage', for that would be neither to her honour nor Elizabeth's nor to Mary's advantage. Nor could she allow her to go to France, for when she had been in France before she had been a pretender to the English throne.

Two or three days after this interview, Elizabeth must have received a letter written by Mary on 21 June in which she enlarged on the points made by Herries and Fleming. She complained of Elizabeth's attitude, threatened to go to France if she could not be heard in person in England and be 'speedily helped' there, and asked for a passport to enable Lord Fleming to go to France, where she professed to be confident of support. There is also an undated letter from Mary to Elizabeth which seems to belong to this period. In it Mary complains of the partiality of Elizabeth's ministers, mentions that Lady Lennox and others have assured her that she will be kept from ever returning to Scotland, points out how unreasonable it was to refuse her access to Elizabeth's presence, where Lady Lennox and others could accuse her face to face, asks for leave to go to the continent and again requests a passport for Fleming. Mary was obviously making the most of her assets. The application for a passport for Fleming was rejected.

It was evident that further efforts would be required to persuade Mary to come to terms. Elizabeth wrote to her on 30 June. She assured Mary that she need not hesitate to answer to a representative of the English crown, not indeed 'judicially' (for that was 'a matter not yet to come'), but in order to assure Elizabeth of her defences, 'for my satisfaction – the thing I most long for'. She added, 'I assure you I will do nothing to hurt you, but rather honour and aid you'. This went a long way to meet Mary's case, but Mary was still thinking in terms of explaining her position to a sister queen, as an equal, not of pleading her cause before a superior, and she said so when she replied to Elizabeth on 13 July. But on the same day as she wrote that letter she was removed from Carlisle, to Bolton on Wensleydale, not in order to be nearer Elizabeth but to lessen the risk that she might escape. Elizabeth was, however, pursuing the matter through Herries as well as in correspondence directly with Mary. She had asked Herries whether Mary would submit the hearing of her cause to her sister queen, and Herries had replied that she would if she were in her own place as a sovereign and native princess, the others as subjects. Elizabeth's parting words to Herries, as he reported them, were that she was Mary's 'loving friend, and would leave nothing undone for her as if the cause was her own – and if she referred the hearing of her case to her, commanded me to say that she would not take it upon her to be a judge, knowing my mistress was a princess, but accept it to dress and agree her and her subjects and put her in her own country again according to God's calling'. This message, which was almost an unqualified promise of restoration, was conveyed to Mary by Herries when he returned on 24 July. He brought Elizabeth's request that Mary should commit her cause to Elizabeth, not thereby making the latter judge over her, 'but rather as her dear cousin and friend to commit herself to her advice and counsel'. If she would do this, Elizabeth would surely set her in 'her seat of regiment and dignity regal'. If Moray and his party proved his charges, the restoration would be conditional on their being secured in their honours and estates, but if they could not prove their case, then Elizabeth would restore Mary absolutely, by force if necessary, on certain conditions.

Mary consented to Elizabeth's proposals, and said so in a letter to her on 28 July. She was not afraid, she declared, to assert her innocence, and agreed that two persons of distinction, chosen by Elizabeth, should meet with Moray or Morton, or both, and some of her own supporters, and that they should treat of her affairs without prejudice to her honour, crown, position or right to the English succession. Mary had perhaps little choice but to agree, for France was as disturbed as ever and Spain was occupied with troubles in the Netherlands. Yet she had been brought to give her consent only with reluctance, and she was displeased by Elizabeth's failure to treat her as favourably as she had hoped; this she stated quite explicitly, in a letter in which she said that if Elizabeth was a lion, she was of the same breed. Mary also realised that agreement to an enquiry involved commanding her followers in Scotland to disregard her earlier command to muster on her behalf, to lay down their arms and to withdraw their application for French help, and it was self-evident that this armistice was bound to be directly favourable to the *de facto* government being carried on by Moray.

To have brought both Moray and Mary to agree to an enquiry was a triumph for English diplomacy. But whether it had been achieved without some dishonesty is debatable. It would be easy to see in the negotiations a design to lull Mary into optimistically submitting to an investigation which might in fact prove detrimental to her and meantime strengthen her opponents in Scotland. Some contemporaries were in no doubt that the ways of the English government were devious if not disingenuous. The Spanish ambassador said, 'They have signs and countersigns, and whilst they publicly write and do one thing, they secretly order another', and one Scot was reported to have complained that 'the Queen of England was using towards his mistress fair words and foul deeds'. Even Knollys seems to have had his suspicions, when he asked Cecil whether it was good 'to halt and dissemble' with Mary. It is in this context, too, that we should see the conjectures that the intention all along was to detain Mary in England indefinitely. Already in July a rumour to this effect had come to the ears of the French and Spanish ambassadors in London: they reported that Elizabeth had no intention of reconciling Mary with her subjects and was more likely to detain her 'in an honourable prison' and in no danger of her life. But, while it is true that to present the prospects of any enquiry in such a way that it would appeal to both Moray and Mary undoubtedly required some sleight of hand, the apparent equivocation on the part of the English government may merely reflect a divergence between Elizabeth and her ministers. It appears, for example, that Cecil sent Moray a message of qualified encouragement and of assurance of support, and this was hard to square with Elizabeth's insistence that Moray's rôle was to defend himself against Mary's accusations. There seems little doubt that Elizabeth was genuinely more favourable to Mary than most of her councillors were. If the idea of detaining her heir presumptive in prison without a fair trial had occurred to Elizabeth at the outset it might not have been surprising, for that had been precisely her own experience when she was heir presumptive to her own sister. But, to do her justice, it seems that she was only slowly and reluctantly driven to this solution, though some of her ministers thought of it earlier. Another point of divergence between Elizabeth and Cecil was this: the Queen was far too sensible to press the argument which Cecil dredged up by resurrecting the pretensions of England to superiority over Scotland.

The attitude of the council was certainly critical of Elizabeth's professed intention to restore Mary. At a consultation of English ministers on 20 June it had been decided that the Queen should 'proceed to be informed of the cause between the Queen of Scots and her subjects' and should neither assist Mary, see her, have her restored nor allow her to leave the realm 'before her cause be honourably tried'. As to the possibility of Mary's restoration on conditions, it was pointed out that it was impracticable to provide any sanctions to ensure that Mary would fulfil such conditions. A paper of the same date, in Cecil's hand, purports to list the considerations 'Pro Regina Scotorum' and those 'Contra Regina Scotorum'. It shows that he already knew the general character of Moray's case, though he makes no mention of written evidence, and he observes that Mary has not had a chance to defend herself although she offers to accuse her subjects who have deposed her of the crimes wherewith she herself is charged. The case this paper makes for Mary rests less on a belief in the possibility of her innocence than on her position as a queen and a refugee and her offer to purge herself and accuse her subjects. Six weeks later, after the conditions proposed for Mary's restoration had been formulated, Cecil wrote disapprovingly of his Queen's attitude: 'The Queen's Majesty . . . meaneth to have the matter between the Queen of Scots and her subjects heard in this realm and compounded, as I think, with a certain manner of restitution of the Queen, and that limited with certain conditions; which how they shall be afterwards performed, wise men may doubt.'

There is no doubt, however, that Cecil and those who thought like him had at least succeeded in restraining Elizabeth from restoring Mary unconditionally. Whichever way the investigation went, Mary was to be restored only on terms. It had been in Cecil's mind from the outset to turn Mary's necessity into England's opportunity and strike an advantageous bargain, for he had held that even should she be acquitted she should make certain concessions 'in consideration of the benefit of acquittal'. Cecil's minutes are a completely cold-blooded assessment of the situation, with no suggestion whatever that there was any question of doing justice or even of being guided by any evidence that might be produced. Therefore, should Elizabeth decide to restore Mary, it would be on three conditions: 'the religion' was to be the same in England as in Scotland, there was to be a bond of amity between the two countries, and Mary was to make no further claims to Elizabeth's throne.

Cecil had his misgivings about the possibility of binding Mary effectively to those, or any, terms, and it was clearly impossible to limit the sovereignty of a ruling monarch. At the same time, the prospect that a restored Mary might fulfil the first condition, relating to uniformity in religion, by fostering the Book of Common Prayer in Scotland, was not wholly illusory. The idea was not even a new one. As far back as February 1562 it had been rumoured in Scotland that Mary had been advised by her liberal-minded uncle, the Cardinal of Lorraine, 'to embrace the religion of England'. And in 1567, not long after Darnley's murder, when Cecil had evidently suggested to Maitland of Lethington that he should influence Mary to 'allow of' the English 'estate in religion', Maitland reported: 'I do not despair but although she will not yield at the first yet with progress of time that point shall be

71

obtained.' Since then, Mary had been married to Bothwell by a Protestant bishop and had taken the Scottish reformed church under her protection. Now, on 8 August 1568, there came a report to Cecil from the puritanical Knollys, who should not have been easy to deceive in such matters: 'Surely the Queen doth seem, outwardly, not only to favour the form, but also the chief articles, of the religion of the gospel, namely justification by faith only; and she heareth the faults of papistry revealed by preaching and otherwise, with contented ears and with gentle and weak replies.' Indeed, Knollys took the prospect of Anglo-Scottish conformity on the Anglican model so seriously that he was alarmed lest it might mean the suppression in Scotland of the 'form of Geneva', on which he personally looked favourably, and he had to acquit himself of the charge that he had tried to prejudice Mary against the Prayer Book. Even after the prospect of her immediate restoration had faded, Mary continued her flirtation with Anglicanism, at the end of February 1569, when she was at Tutbury, it was reported that she 'heard the English service with a book of the psalms in English in her hand'. It was a very different Mary who, on the scaffold at Fotheringhay in 1587, rejected the prayers of the Dean of Peterborough.

Moray was sceptical about the sincerity of Mary's professions: 'Her resorting to the service of the Church of England serves her turn presently to move godly men to conceive a good opinion of her conformity and towardness. But I fear being restored to her government again . . . it should be one of the most difficult conditions to become good for, that she should abandon the mass.' One detects Moray's tight-lipped censoriousness: the man's conscious rectitude must have been insufferable. But he was quite right in seeing the whole thing as a piece of opportunism on Mary's part, for she was quite candid about it herself. When some of her Roman Catholic friends expressed alarm about what she was doing she took care to reassure them of her adherence to Rome, as Knollys reported on 21 September: 'she openly professed herself of the Papists' religion more earnestly than before . . . And to me alone, when I misliked this, she said, "Why, would you have me to lose France and Spain and all my friends in other places, by seeming to change my religion, and yet I am not assured that the Queen my good sister will be my assured friend to the satisfaction of my honour and expectation?" ' Mary's calculation that she could not afford to alienate her continental friends without more definite assurance for her future than Elizabeth had yet given was justified: indeed, on the very day before Mary made the reaffirmation of her attachment to Rome Elizabeth had written to Moray denying the allegation by Mary's supporters that she would be restored in any event and promising that if she were found guilty she would not be restored. Yet Mary's equivocal and opportunist policy continued, for her instructions to her commissioners, dated on 29 September, a week after her declaration of her fidelity to Rome, contained an undertaking to consider conformity with England.

The somewhat ambiguous situation and the uncertainty about the future which had been reflected in the correspondence planning the investigation continued to dominate events when the conference finally opened, at York in October. It may be doubted if any even of the principals really wanted the enquiry to be pushed to a decisive conclusion. Mary, indeed, may well have hoped for a vindication and her unconditional restoration, but, if she realised that to be unlikely, she was bound to prefer an equivocal outcome to an unqualified condemnation as a criminal. Besides, she must have wondered how she might fare if she went back to Scotland, necessarily to rely on some faction, and she can hardly have believed that she had many supporters who were altruistic enough to put her welfare before their own. She may even have reflected that it might on the whole be more to her advantage to remain in England – provided it was on terms which gave her some freedom of action – and exploit her claims to the English throne in order to build up a party which might in the end win two kingdoms for her. Elizabeth, even without Cecil's patient analysis of the 'dangers' inherent in various possibilities, and even apart from her constitutional irresolution, had to gain from an outcome which neither restored a rival nor justified a sentence on a sister queen. She probably aimed at some kind of compromise which would save Mary from condemnation but at the same time maintain Moray's government in Scotland, preferably with Mary restored to nominal sovereignty. Moray, the third of the principals, remained uneasy about the future of his person, property and authority should he publicly accuse Mary of murder and then find the charge not sustained and Mary restored. Apart from his apprehension on this score, he wanted his government to continue, which it could do with indubitable legality only if Mary would accept a settlement involving its recognition. It was reported that, just before the conference at York opened, Moray sent an agent to Mary to seek her agreement to a compromise whereby she would have a large allowance and remain in England, while Moray continued in office as regent. One of the English commissioners at York – the Earl of Sussex – thought that if only Mary would agree to surrender the crown voluntarily and continue to live in England, Moray's party would 'forbear to touch her honour' and perhaps even publicly absolve her. So far were they from any interest in justice for its own sake.

If the principals were thus hesitant, some of their agents had their own reasons for not wanting to push matters to extremes. Possibly not a single one of the commissioners who assembled at York* was quite clear in his own mind about what he hoped to achieve, and it may even be doubted if any one of them was wholly convinced of the righteousness of the action he was taking. On Moray's side, Maitland of Lethington wanted a reconciliation which would lead to Mary's restoration, partly because he looked above all to her recognition as heir to England – which a condemned murderess could not hope for – and partly because he feared discolsures of his own participation in a plot against Darnley. It was remarked that he wanted matters to be ended 'in dulce manner', and he was conspicuously active in pressing for a composition. As for Herries, on Mary's side, he was willing to swear to say nothing but what was just and true, but not to swear to all that he knew to be true: he was prepared, in short, to tell the truth, but not the whole truth. So he, like Maitland, 'laboured for a reconciliation without odious accusations'. If the attitude of Herries suggests that Mary's representatives had no real confidence in their mistress's innocence, it finds support in what Lesley, another of Mary's commissioners, said about her – admittedly three years later: she had, he said, poisoned her first husband, consented to the murder of the second, married the murderer and then brought him to the field [at Carberry] to be murdered. A triple murderess. The Englishman who heard Mary's ambassador – as Lesley then was – make this statement commented, 'Lord, what people are these, what a Queen and what an ambassador'.

There was as much doubt and hesitation, though of a different kind, among Elizabeth's commissioners as there was among Moray's and Mary's. Sir Ralph Sadler went to York an unhappy and perplexed man. 'Who is a tyrant?' he asked Cecil; 'who may depose a tyrant?' And he wondered whether Mary should be held to be bound by the abdication which had been extorted from her in prison. The answers to such questions, he realised, had implications for England, indeed for all realms, and to deal with them required legal knowledge. Yet his fellow commissioners, the Duke

---

* In Chapter 4 particulars are given of the commissioners who represented the three parties at York and of their proceedings there.

of Norfolk and the Earl of Sussex, though they were wise and discreet, 'of their learning in the laws you can judge', while he, for his part, was 'utterly unlearned in all kinds of learning'. Looking ahead to the conclusion which the conference might reach, he observed that if the decision should be that Mary should have the title of Queen of Scots while others had the power, 'I see not how it can hang together . . . Surely it cannot long continue'.

Norfolk, head of the English commission, was appalled by his task, and told Cecil that he saw nothing but difficulties: 'This cause is the doubtfulest and dangerest that ever I dealt in: if you saw and heard the constant affirming of both sides, not without great stoutness, you would wonder.' Not the least of Norfolk's troubles arose from the fact that he was a fair-minded man, and fair-mindedness was perhaps not a qualification for his task. Thus he was enough of a realist to appreciate Moray's difficulty, and was inclined to support the Regent's demand for guarantees before he accused Mary: 'They stand for their lives, lands and goods, and they are not ignorant if they would, for it is every day told them that as long as they abstain from touching their Queen's honour she will make them what reasonable end they can devise: it were pity that they for too much trusting to us should hinder their own cause.' It was characteristic of Norfolk's fairness that he found it hard to see any valid reason for rejecting Mary's claim to be heard in person; should she 'in the end be driven to her trial' and desired to be present, the request would be 'a thing in my opinion that needs good consideration'. Norfolk also saw far enough into the Scottish situation to appreciate the difficulty of finding a settlement which would satisfy all the factions, and he took a poor view of the single-mindedness of the commissioners. Mary, he thought, had better friends on the Regent's side than on her own, and, while 'some few in this company' meant 'plainly and truly', others sought wholly to serve their own private ends, caring not 'what becomes neither of Queen nor King'.

Presently, however, Norfolk, like others, began to have his own private ends. On 16 October he had a long conference with Lethington. The latter would certainly urge on Norfolk his own preference for a compromise solution, and Norfolk disclosed to Lethington his own belief that Elizabeth's purpose was not to 'end' Mary's cause at this time, but to hold it in suspense, yet to have Mary so discredited through Moray's revelations that she could be detained in England for some time, until the storm blew over and Elizabeth could show her favour. It would appear, too, that after this conference with Maitland, Norfolk discussed with Moray the possibility of a compromise settlement and impressed on him the danger he incurred by accusing Mary. If, however, there is anything in the theory that Lethington had told Norfolk that the Casket Letters were not genuine, Norfolk's own view may well have been that Mary ought not to accept a compromise but should press for a triumphant acquittal and unconditional restoration.

It has been suggested that it was Lethington, in his talk with Norfolk on 16 October, who first implanted in Norfolk's mind the idea that he might marry Mary. But, although Norfolk may not have been an over-intelligent man, it did not take much originality to think of this. That speculation about the possibility of Mary's remarriage was becoming current is indicated in a letter which Sir Francis Knollys wrote to Norfolk from London on 14 or 15 October. Knollys had gone to court, perhaps as the bearer of a report by Norfolk from York dated 11 October, and on his way south, he relates, he 'mused' on the possibility of a reconciliation through a 'stay' of the publication of 'odious accusations' against Mary. He reflected that Elizabeth could either, on a 'full hearing', detain Mary and maintain the government of Scotland in name of King James, or else stay the publication of the accusations and make a reconciliation. When he saw Elizabeth, she said to him that her commissioners would not 'begin severely', but if Moray and his party would 'fall to extremities, they shall be answered roundly and at the full, and then we are past all reconciliation'. Knollys persisted in his view that if there were no open publication to the world of Mary's guilt she could be brought to outward reconciliation, and he wondered if she could be married to his kinsman George Carey, the son of Elizabeth's cousin Lord Hunsdon. This, he reflected, would avoid any marriage with 'the Hamiltons or with the French'. A few days later, writing to Cecil that he did not see how Elizabeth could with honour and safety detain Mary unless the latter should be 'utterly disgraced to the world', he said that, on the other hand, a necessary condition of her restoration ought to be that 'all foreign practices be avoided by an English marriage'. It is noticeable that even Knollys, godly man that he was, did not see guilt in a queen as an obstacle to respectable matrimony. Knollys, who had the advantage over Norfolk of immediate contract with the captive, seems to have put his ideas before Mary, and he learned that she would not 'greatly mislike' a marriage with a near kinsman of Elizabeth on her mother's side. This was on 20 October, and on the 21st Mary was indicating a readiness to be divorced from Bothwell. She was ready to grasp at an English marriage as she was ready to grasp at the English Prayer Book.

So far as Norfolk's own schemes were concerned, his negotiations with Moray had been discovered by Morton, who told Cecil. No doubt from Cecil the news reached Elizabeth, who was soon, early in November, to have an opportunity to challenge the Duke about his marriage plans. Norfolk protested that he would rather go to the Tower than marry Mary, with whom 'he could not be sure of his pillow'. He had perhaps been listening to Lesley telling how she had disposed of two husbands and had tried to dispose of a third. But his plans were serious enough, and this, be it noted, was after he had been shown, in confidence, the Casket Letters, one of which he characterised as 'horrible'. Of course, if Maitland had told Norfolk that the letters were really forgeries, they were no obstacle, but it is quite unnecessary to make this postulation. After all, Knollys was convinced of Mary's guilt, yet was willing to see her married to his own kinsman, and Norfolk was unlikely to have been more scrupulous. The fact that Mary was a queen outweighed other considerations, and once more it is evident that there was little concern whether she was guilty or innocent. Moray was to admit a year later that he had dealt with Norfolk, who had pointed out the advantage of another marriage for Mary, so that she would have more children, and had made his own ambitions plain.

The one thing that all the speculation about Mary's remarriage achieved seems to have been a hardening in Elizabeth's attitude. She seems now to have been awakened as never before to the danger from Mary, and from this point became more hostile. Norfolk told Moray that the Queen regarded the continued existence of Bothwell as a useful safeguard against Mary's remarriage. Cecil wrote jubilantly on 24 October: 'The Queen's Majesty is now at the pinch so careful of her own surety and state as I perceive the Queen of Scots shall not be advanced to greater credit than her cause will serve.' It may well have been not only news of Norfolk's ambiguous proceedings at York, but a hardening of Elizabeth's own attitude, which led her to move the proceedings to Westminster from York, where on the whole, as we shall see, Mary's case had made a good showing.

In addition to Mary, Moray and Elizabeth, there were two other parties who considered themselves entitled to a voice in the proceedings to determine Mary's future. They were all along on the fringe of the enquiry, and no decision was likely to be made which did not take their interests into account. One was the house of Lennox, the other the house of Hamilton.

The head of the house of Lennox, Darnley's father, who had

been designated prosecutor of Bothwell in the previous year, might have been expected to have a case already prepared on the subject of his son's murder, and he was early in the field. It has been suggested that as early as 28 May he gave to Elizabeth a 'Narrative' of the crime which he had drawn up during the preceding days, though it seems that he was at this stage acting essentially as an agent of Moray, under the encouragement of John Wood. Then, on 11 June, he wrote to Scotland asking for a lot of information which he might have been thought to have at hand already, e.g., 'How soon was the King [Darnley] put in the house of Kirk o' Field, how long before it was prepared, by whose command? . . . How long the King lay in Kirk o' Field before that execution and horrible murder; who accompanied the Queen ordinarily when she visited him at Kirk o' Field?' The only original feature in the curious catalogue was some questions about the behaviour of the Archbishop of St Andrews, John Hamilton, which suggest that Lennox aimed at throwing suspicion on the house of Hamilton. Lennox, at any rate, was clearly gathering ammunition for a full indictment, though not necessarily with a view to taking part himself in the expected investigation. Had he pressed a claim to do so, it would have been difficult for the English government to turn him down out of hand: not only was the murdered man his son, but his wife was Elizabeth's cousin and the first princess of the royal house of England. As Lennox said on 18 August, when he reminded Cecil that he and his wife had sent to Elizabeth a supplication requesting justice for Darnley's murder, he was 'the party whom the matter toucheth nearest and whose appearance may be thought most necessary' at any enquiry. However, despite this plea, the general impression probably was that Lennox was rather tiresome, and Elizabeth refused, on 25 August, to allow him to attend the enquiry. He was not represented at York, but was ultimately allowed to appear at Westminster on 29 November, when he presented an accusation of Mary, on three sheets of paper, along with two letters written to Mary and two written by her. His intervention had no influence on events.

The Hamiltons had a double interest. In the first place, while they were unquestionably the heirs presumptive of Mary, it was not so clear that they were the heirs of James, for it was argued that, as Darnley had been King, the succession to James passed to his paternal kinsmen and his heir was Darnley's brother Charles. It was therefore contrary to Hamilton policy to recognise James as King. Secondly, it was contended for the Hamiltons that the office of regent, should there be a regent, ought to be held by the heir presumptive, the head of their house. Moray's case for assuming the regency rested on the argument that the office was elective, but clearly Lennox also could advance a claim to the regency if his son were heir presumptive to James.* All the time the enquiry was being planned, and while it was being held, the head of the Hamiltons, the Duke of Châtelherault, was in London, and although he was one of the most ineffective of men, he could not be ignored. The Duke of Norfolk, with his usual fair-mindedness, considered that the Hamiltons were as 'good' as any other Scottish faction and that it would be hard to make Châtelherault come to terms with any rival for authority in Scotland as long as his own claims to the regency stood and as long as he had his second son, Lord John Hamilton, in mind as a future spouse of Mary. Cecil, on the other hand, was always very hostile to the Hamiltons. In the first assessment he had made of the situation, he had seen it as one of the disadvantages of allowing Mary to return to Scotland that the Hamiltons would be 'exalted'. Here, as in many other things, he was at issue with his Queen. Elizabeth always showed a marked tenderness for the Hamiltons: one wonders if she was enough of a woman to be moved by pity for the fate of Châtelherault's eldest son, the young Earl of Arran, who had once been her suitor (as well as Mary's) and the young hopeful of many Scottish and English Protestants but who had been confined as a lunatic since 1562.

However many interests were involved, and whatever weight the various arguments might have, the power to come to a decision rested with the English government and no one else, if only because it had *de facto* control of Mary's person. Consequently, the outcome of the investigations was bound to depend in the long run more on William Cecil and his mistress than on any of the persons who assembled at York. But it was some time before even Cecil saw a way of resolving the many difficulties he had discerned from the outset. On the very day (16 October) when Norfolk, in York, was shaking his head over the 'doubtfulest and dangerest' cause, Cecil sent the Duke a minute which was equally full of doubts and dangers. He asked whether it was reasonable that Elizabeth, as superior of Scotland, should hear and determine the causes between Mary and her subjects. If Mary should be found guilty, could she be restored to Scotland with security for her life, to live either as Queen Dowager or at titular Queen, with James as King? What kind of guarantee could be given to Moray? How could Châtelherault be reconciled to allow of the government of Scot-

* For the arguments on these issues, see pp. 92–3 below.

land, in case the Queen be found guilty? What was the opinion in Scotland as to the succession if the prince should die and the Queen have no further issue? If Mary should be found guilty and remain in England, what allowance would Scotland give for her maintenance? If she should not be found guilty, how could the prince and his adherents be assured of their lives? The problems were manifold, but one feels that the difficulties Cecil notes as likely to arise from Mary's continued detention in England – the conciliation of the Hamiltons and some finance from Scotland towards Mary's maintenance – were demonstrably less serious than those in the way of her return to Scotland.

A little more than a month later, on 21 November, Cecil drafted another memorandum on possible courses of action. 'The best way for England, but not the easiest', was that 'the Queen of Scots remain deprived of her crown and the state continue as it is'. The alternative which Cecil gives is described by him as 'profitable for England and not so hard', but in fact it is difficult to believe that he was so insensitive as to put it forward seriously, and easier to believe that he set it forth to reinforce his preference for the first alternative. The proposal was that Mary should be induced to accept joint sovereignty with James and that the government of Scotland should be committed to a council selected by Elizabeth from a list drawn up half by Mary and half by the Earl and Countess of Lennox. Meantime Moray was to continue his government. A parliament was to be summoned in the names of Mary and James. Twenty-four hostages should be delivered into England, twelve of Mary's party, named by Moray, and twelve of Moray's, named by Mary, to remain for three months after the parliament, as pledges of peace. The parliament was to define the Scottish succession or else to declare that Châtelherault had still such rights as he had when Mary married Darnley. Mary was to remain in England for twelve months after the parliament, and not to depart without Elizabeth's licence; and James, it was suggested, might be brought to England for his education. Conyers Read described those proposals as 'so fantastic as to be almost ludicrous' and adds that it would have been hard to find any Scotsman of any party who would have accepted them.

The most illuminating commentary on the whole situation, written on 22 October, when the proceedings at York were petering out, came from the third of the English commissioners, the Earl of Sussex, evidently in reply to the questions which Cecil had indicated in his minute of the 16th. Sussex observed that 'this great matter . . . must at length take end, either by finding the Scots

Queen guilty of the crimes that are objected against her or by some manner of composition with a show of saving her honour'. The first, he thought, would hardly be attempted, mainly because Mary would retort by accusing the 'adverse party' or most of them of 'manifest consent to the murder', and 'her proofs will judicially fall best out, as it is thought'. The probability was that efforts would be made instead for a 'composition'. Moray and his party wanted Mary to surrender her crown voluntarily to her son and confirm the regency to Moray, on the understanding that the Hamiltons would be admitted to his council, while Mary remained in England, with her French dowry and perhaps 'a portion out of Scotland'. If so, they would 'put her in hope, not only to receive her again to her royal estate if her son die, but also, upon some proof of the forgetting of her displeasure, to procure in short time that she may be restored in her son's life and he to give place to her for her life'. Should she not agree, Moray would consent to her detention in England, while he remained regent. The Hamiltons, for their part, wanted the Queen to be restored to her crown and to return to Scotland, but were 'contented', in respect of her misgovernment, that she should be controlled by 'a council of the nobility of that realm' under Elizabeth's surveillance. By way of ensuring that this arrangement would endure, Mary was to have only 'certain houses of no force', while the castles of Edinburgh, Stirling and Dunbar and other principal fortresses were to be delivered into the hands of 'upright noblemen that leaned to no faction'. They would agree to the bringing up of the prince in England, and might even be induced to consent to Mary's remaining in England while she was invested with nominal sovereignty.

Sussex's conclusion was emphatic: 'I think surely no end can be made good for England except the person of the Scots Queen be detained, by one means or other, in England.' Of the two possible outcomes of the enquiry, he thought the first – Mary's condemnation – preferable 'if Moray will produce such matter as the Queen's Majesty may, by virtue of her superiority over Scotland, find the Scots Queen guilty of the murder of her husband, and therewith detain her in England at the charges of Scotland, and allow of the crowning of the young King and the regency of Moray'. If Châtelherault would agree, his title to the succession should be acknowledged; if not, Moray ought to be assisted to suppress him and his adherents. Sussex feared, however, that judicial proofs would not be adequate, and if so it would be necessary, after all, to proceed by way of composition. If Mary would not voluntarily surrender, then her restoration should be merely nominal, she remaining in England and James being brought there, while Moray remained regent and an attempt was made to conclude an agreement between him and the Hamiltons, so that the latter would not turn to France; but if Hamilton would not come to terms, he was to be prosecuted by confiscation of his property.

Sussex, like his chief, Norfolk, was a fair-minded man, to the extent at least that he appreciated the importance of all the conflicting interests. But he also, like Cecil, had the advantage of England much at heart. He was more realistic than Cecil, but in the end not decisive enough to be helpful.

4. The Enquiry:
The Proceedings at York

The intricate diplomacy required to bring Mary and Moray to agree to a confrontation at an enquiry, as well perhaps as the complex and sometimes conflicting thoughts in the minds of Elizabeth and her advisers, caused the opening of the enquiry to be deferred to a date much later than had at first been proposed. As late as the end of June it had been intended that 'some end may ensue before the 1st of August', but this was quite unrealistic. On 22 July Elizabeth wrote to Moray with some urgency, asking him to postpone the parliament which he had planned for the following month and to make all the speed he could, so that either he himself or others on his behalf would be ready to come to either Newcastle or Durham. On 18 August it was thought that proceedings would start at the beginning of September, but this clearly allowed far too little time and it was not until 29 August that Elizabeth herself named her commissioners. The choice of York, in preference to any other place in the north, must have been made by that time.

It was early in September, when it was believed that the 25th of that month was the appointed date of meeting, that arrangements began to be made by Moray and by Mary. On 3 September Moray's secretary asked the English government for safe-conducts for Moray himself, the Earls of Morton and Glencairn, the Bishop of Orkney, the Commendator of Dunfermline and Lord Lindsay, with a hundred horse, and four days later Moray himself made the same request. Moray went ahead with his arrangements, pending the arrival of the safe-conduct. On 16 September he gave a receipt to Morton for the Casket and its contents, and on the 18th a commission was issued, in King James's name, authorising Moray, Morton, Orkney, Dunfermline and Lindsay to meet Elizabeth's commissioners at York and to declare the causes why the confederate lords had taken up arms. It can, however, be assumed that Moray and his party remained at home until the arrival of the safe-conduct (which was issued by the English government on 16 September), and they do not seem to have left Edinburgh until about the 25th. They were in Berwick on the 28th.

It is noticeable that of the three principals – Mary, Elizabeth and Moray – Moray was the only one who went to York in person. Nominally, of course, he was a commissioner for the infant King James, but in practice he had the advantage over the other parties at York that he did not have to refer back for instructions. The Earl of Morton, who accompanied him, was unquestionably the second in command among the anti-Marian lords in Scotland, and had indeed been designated as regent should Moray decline the office. He had all along been unswerving in his attachment to the Reformation and the English alliance, and was a man in whom resolution passed into ruthlessness. Adam Bothwell, Bishop of Orkney since 1559, had declared for the reformation in 1560 and had done good work for the reformed church in his diocese, but had recently been forced to surrender his bishopric property in exchange for that of the abbey of Holyrood, resigned in his favour by Lord Robert Stewart. He had played a conspicuous part in some recent events, for he had officiated at the marriage of Mary to the Earl of Bothwell, he had served on the expedition which pursued Bothwell to the north, and he had anointed King James at his coronation. Robert Pitcairn, Archdeacon of St Andrews and Commendator of Dunfermline, was a man of less note, but had been a member of the privy council. Patrick, sixth Lord Lindsay, had been one of the murderers of Rizzio and was the man who had laid hands on the Queen at Lochleven when she showed reluctance to sign her deed of abdication.

Besides the named commissioners, the following also accompanied Moray as professional advisers or assessors: James MacGill of Nether Rankeillor, a lawyer who had held the office of Clerk Register (that is, keeper of the official archives of the kingdom) since 1554 except for a period between his dismissal by Mary in February 1566 and his reinstatement by Moray in 1567; Henry Balnaves of Halhill, another lawyer, who had shared John Knox's imprisonment in the French galleys and had written a treatise on Justification by Faith; George Buchanan, the scholar of European renown who had at one time entertained Mary by reading Livy with her after dinner but who was a client of the Lennox family and had turned virulently against Mary after the murder of Darnley, the heir of Lennox; and William Maitland of Lethington, who had been secretary of state since December 1558. When we recall that Bishop Bothwell was also a lawyer and a judge of the court of session, we appreciate the remark of Sir Ralph Sadler, on the English side, that 'It is meet that we go well prepared with learned men, for be assured the Scots will bring such'. He realised that Elizabeth's team was no match for Moray's in legal skill.

Mary's commissioners seem in the first instance to have been nominated not by her personally but by a meeting at Dumbarton on 12 September, when her supporters, to the number of seven earls, twelve lords, eight bishops and eight commendators, drew up a defence against the allegations of the confederate lords. Mary had presumably been informed of the selection made by this gathering when, on 15 September, Knollys forwarded to his government a request from her for passports for the Earl of Cassilis, the Bishops of Ross and Galloway, Lords Herries and Boyd, Sir John Gordon of Lochnivar and Sir James Cockburn of Skirling. However, a change was subsequently made, for when, a fortnight later, Mary issued her commission the men she named were the Bishop of Ross, Lords Livingston, Boyd and Herries, the Commendator of Kilwinning and the lairds of Lochinvar and Skirling. The terms of the commission followed the lines of a statement drawn up at Dumbarton on the 12th: there is a defence, or at least a denial of the charges against the Queen; and a statement that 'there are divers in Scotland, both men and women, that can counterfeit my handwriting and write the like manner of writing which I use as well as myself' anticipated the evidence which Moray's party was expected to produce.

It is evident beyond all doubt, from the composition of the Dumbarton conference and from the membership of Mary's commission, that her cause was not that of a friendless refugee. It may be very much doubted if Moray could have mustered a gathering of as many notables as assembled at Dumbarton to support the Queen, and the commissioners who went to York on her behalf were not undistinguished. John Lesley had been the 'official' (that is, the bishop's judicial deputy) in the diocese of Aberdeen before 1560, and had become a lord of session in 1564 and Mary had nominated him to the bishopric of Ross at the beginning of 1567. Lord Livingston, brother of one of the Queen's 'Maries', was devoted to the Queen, but he was a Protestant and Mary had shown him and his wife the special favour of attending a Protestant sermon after the baptism of their child in 1565. Lord Boyd had been active as one of the insurgent 'lords of the congregation' in 1559–60, he had supported Moray's rebellion after the Darnley marriage in 1565 and had joined the confederacy of lords formed to 'liberate' Mary from Bothwell. Lord Herries, like Boyd, had been an active insurgent in 1559, but from 1565 he had tended to support Mary rather than the Protestant party. Gavin Hamilton had been Commendator of Kilwinning since 1550, and since 1551 he had also been coadjutor of the archbishopric of St Andrews (with a view to keeping that lucrative and influential position in the hands of the Hamilton family after the death of Archbishop John Hamilton). He had become a lord of session in 1555 and in the crisis of 1559–60 had given a cautious support to the reformers which suggests either that he was by temperament something of a trimmer or that he and the Archbishop had deliberately decided to take different lines so that, whichever way the revolt ended, the family interest would be secure. Sir John Gordon of Lochinvar had been a reformer in 1560, but had supported Mary against Moray in 1565. Cockburn of Skirling had played little part in affairs, but the Cockburn family as a whole was Protestant; on the other hand, he had evidently continued to serve Mary during the period of her 'thraldom' to Bothwell. What is especially significant of those commissioners is that not one of them could be described as a Roman Catholic. Even Lesley, who is usually so regarded, told Knollys that he had always been 'quiet' in religion, and Knollys reported that he 'seems almost a Protestant'. Some of Mary's other commissioners had had conspicuous records as supporters of the reformed church. It cannot be stressed too strongly that opinion for and against Mary had not divided along religious lines; and this means, incidentally, that the English attitude to the Marian party was not necessarily going to be decided primarily by religious considerations. A striking illustration of the way in which Scottish opinion had divided is the fact that the Bishop of Orkney, who appeared as a commissioner for Moray, and the Bishop of Galloway, who was one of the nominees of Mary's supporters, were now on opposite sides although their careers hitherto had been remarkably similar and each had carried through the reformation in his diocese. Yet, while Mary's commissioners represented a wide range of interests and were not undistinguished, only Lesley and Gavin Hamilton were professional men. If Moray could muster the expertise, Mary on the whole had blood, birth and breeding on her side.

Elizabeth's commissioners had been nominated on 29 August. The first of them was the Duke of Norfolk, the only English duke and first subject of the realm. If Elizabeth was not attending in person, Norfolk was the obvious man to lead the delegation. But it may not have escaped notice that Norfolk had acted for Elizabeth in Scottish affairs once before, when he negotiated the Treaty of

Berwick with the Scottish reforming and anti-French party in February 1560, and one wonders whether his re-appearance now conveyed a hint that England might once more do a deal with a revolutionary Scottish administration. Norfolk was accompanied by Sir Ralph Sadler, a veteran who had served in Anglo-Scottish negotiations in 1543 and again in 1559–60 and must have known Scotland as well as any Englishman did, and by the Earl of Sussex, who had no previous experience of Scottish business but had been conspicuously successful in Elizabeth's service elsewhere.

Detailed instructions, directing these English commissioners how to conduct the enquiry, were drawn up about 24 September. Each side was first to be heard separately, beginning with Mary's representatives, and before the commissioners treated with both sides together they were to consider certain possible outcomes. Thus, if Moray alleged that, although he had proof of Mary's guilt, he felt it inexpedient to charge her with murder lest she should nonetheless be restored, they were to declare that, should the proof of her guilt be plain, Elizabeth would surely think her unworthy of a kingdom; this was in accordance with the undertaking given by Elizabeth to Moray in a letter of 20 September. If, however, there was no conclusive proof, but only suspicions and conjectures which damaged Mary's reputation, Elizabeth would consider how to restore her 'without danger of relapse'. In the event of a decision for her restoration, there would be a treaty to which Elizabeth, Mary and James would all be parties, providing both for the internal affairs of Scotland and for Anglo-Scottish relations. In Scotland there was to be oblivion for past offences, the appointment of a great council to advise Mary, a ban on her marriage without the consent of the estates, the punishment of Bothwell and the establishment of the reformed church. The future relations of Scotland with England were to be determined by a modification of the Treaty of Edinburgh, to enable Mary or her children to take the title and arms of England after Elizabeth's death, and by a league between the two countries, providing for the cessation of Scottish assistance to rebels in Ireland and for a settlement of the 'debatable land' on the Border. Besides, an effort was to be made to have James sent to England, ostensibly to secure his safety, and in the event of complaints in Scotland about failure to fulfil the terms of the treaty appeal was to lie to Elizabeth.

It is perhaps somewhat remarkable that, in the state of sixteenth-century communications, the three parties of commissioners – Elizabeth's from London, Moray's from Edinburgh and Mary's from Bolton – arrived at York within a few hours of each other:

Mary's on the evening on 2 October, Moray and his party the following day and Elizabeth's about an hour behind them.

Preliminaries started on 4 October and lasted for three days. Elizabeth's commissioners, following their instructions, sent first for Mary's representatives, read their own commission from Elizabeth and asked to see Mary's commission. It turned out to be unexpectedly brief, and a fuller version was promised. While this was awaited, Moray and his party, on the 5th, agreed to a form of oath. When Mary's fuller commission was produced, on the 6th, it was found that its preamble contained an assumption that Elizabeth had undertaken to restore Mary and that, while it empowered the commissioners to treat on all things tending to reduce Mary's subjects to obedience it did not authorise them to treat on the cause of the rebellion. A further difficulty arose from the reluctance of Mary's commissioners to follow the example of Moray's and go on oath. It was at this point that Herries declared that he would swear to say nothing but what was just and true, but would not swear to say all in the matter that he knew to be true. Therefore, while Elizabeth's commissioners and Moray's were duly sworn, Mary's were granted time to consider.

On the 7th, when proceedings began in earnest, there was protest and counter-protest – one by Mary's representatives that they did not intend their action to mean that Mary recognised herself as subject to any judge on earth and one by the English commissioners asserting the superiority of the crown of England over Scotland. The atmosphere, nevertheless, was friendly, with 'merry and pleasant speeches'. This is not surprising, for the Scots all knew each other well through long association in the past and had often been of one mind then although they were divided now; besides, Scots generally were accustomed to differ on principles and policies without feeling any personal animosity against one another. On the English side, Sadler must have been an old acquaintance of many of the Scots. Mary's commissioners now took an oath undertaking to declare the causes why they had taken up arms on behalf of their sovereign, but affirming that Mary was a sovereign princess who acknowledged no judge; and Moray's commissioners swore to declare the causes why they had taken up arms against Mary and had deposed her. As planned, it was acknowledged that since Mary was the plaintiff her representatives were to be heard first and Moray was later to have an opportunity to justify his conduct. The hearing therefore started with a statement by word of mouth from Lord Herries, narrating the rebellion against the Queen, her imprisonment and deposition and Moray's assumption of the regency. Bishop Lesley 'briefly and pithily' seconded him. The statement which Herries had thus made orally was given up in writing next day, the 9th, over the signatures of Ross, Livingston, Boyd, Herries, Skirling and Kilwinning.

Moray asked for time to frame a reply to this 'Book of Complaints' as it was called, and did not at once produce evidence against Mary. He had had ample time to prepare a case, but the uncertainty as to how the enquiry would go and as to whether he would have guarantees for his security which he had asked for makes it unlikely that he was equipped with a ready-made statement. No doubt, as a result of the labours of Buchanan and Lennox, provisional productions, suitable to insert into an indictment, were in existence, but probably nothing that could be put forward without amendment. As long as the proceedings at York lasted Moray was concerned, publicly at least, only to justify his own rebellion, and this he attempted to do by laying his emphasis on Mary's marriage to Bothwell when he was under suspicion as Darnley's murderer, and on Mary's failure to prosecute Bothwell. At this stage, on 8 October, he recited Mary's refusal to abandon Bothwell and recalled her 'voluntary' abdication. He said that he had hitherto been disposed to conceal Mary's infamy and he insisted that, before he disclosed it, he must know in what way, if he could prove his charges, his party would be protected against Mary's displeasure and the young King's safety would be assured. He also said that he would not proceed to an accusation of Mary until he had a guarantee that if she were found guilty she would not be restored. Norfolk agreed to this by word of mouth, echoing the clause in his instructions which stated that if Mary were found guilty Elizabeth would think her 'unworthy of a kingdom', but Moray was not satisfied with this and insisted on a written guarantee, especially as Mary's supporters were claiming to have an undertaking that she would be restored in any event.

Next day, the 9th, Moray pressed his point further by asking for a definite answer on four heads: (1) Did the English commissioners have authority to pronounce a verdict on Mary's part in the murder? (2) If so, could they do so without delay once the evidence was presented? (3) If Mary were found guilty, would she be turned over to the Scots or 'such order put to her person' in England that James and his government would be secure? (4) If she were found guilty, would England recognise the government of King James? This seems to have been something of a private approach by Moray, without the collaboration of his fellow commissioners and assessors, among whom only Maitland knew of it. Norfolk could only repeat what he had already said, and give provisional answers, pending consultation with his Queen, to whom he wrote on the same day. No answer was forthcoming as long as proceedings at York continued, and this inevitably made them inconclusive, for Moray continued to defer his full-scale indictment.

All that happened publicly on the 10th was the production by Moray of a written statement, signed by Morton, Adam Bothwell, Lord Lindsay and Dunfermline, offering a defence along the lines he had already indicated by word of mouth on the 8th – Mary's marriage to Bothwell, 'that godless and ambitious man', and her 'voluntary' abdication. But on the same day an additional and startling step was taken at an unofficial level: the Casket Letters were shown privately to the English commissioners. Norfolk described the event in a letter to Elizabeth. Lethington, Mac-Gill, Buchanan and Balnaves approached the Duke and his colleagues 'in private and secret conference with us, not as commissioners, as they protested, but for our better instruction', and produced 'such matter as they have to condemn the Queen of Scots of the murder of her husband, to the intent they would know of us how your majesty understanding the same would judge of the sufficiency of the matter and whether in your majesty's opinion the same will extend to condemn the Queen of Scots of the said murder'. Norfolk gave his Queen a long description of the papers and made it plain that he and his colleagues had been shocked, especially by 'one horrible and long letter of her own hand, as they say, containing foul matter and abominable to be either thought of or to be written by a prince, with divers fond ballads of her own hand. . . . The said letters and ballads to discover such inordinate love between her and Bothwell, her loathesomeness and abhorring of her husband . . . as every good and godly man cannot but detest and abhor the same.' The Scots, he said, were ready to swear to Mary's handwriting and to allege that the matter contained in the papers was such as could hardly be invented or devised by anyone other than Mary, 'for that they discourse of some things which were unknown to any other than to herself and Bothwell'; but he did not commit himself wholly to the belief that the letters were genuine. The action taken on Moray's behalf at this point was in a sense an extension of his demand for a guarantee against the restoration of a guilty Queen, but it was very like an attempt to extract a judgement in advance of a public hearing. It is to be noted that the Scots who approached Norfolk with the letters were none of them, strictly speaking, commissioners, and Moray could no doubt have repudiated their action if he had found it expedient to do so. It is not clear if the deed was meant to be kept secret, but it appears to have become known to Lesley and Boyd on Mary's side.

On 12 October, Herries and Boyd 'conferred in talk' with Elizabeth's commissioners concerning Moray's answer to the 'Book of Complaints', and asked for 'respite in their replication', or time to frame a reply. On the 13th, Elizabeth's commissioners asked Mary's commissioners to have their commission expanded, and Herries agreed to send to Mary for her approval this additional clause: 'to treat, conclude and determine of all other matters and causes whatsoever in controversy between her and her subjects'. On the 14th, Moray seems to have repeated his answer to the 'Book of Complaints', with an express assertion of his right to 'eik' or add to his statement.

On the 16th there came from Mary's side their 'replication', that is, their answer to Moray's formal defence against their own original accusation or 'Book of Complaints'. It was produced in writing, over the signature of all Mary's commissioners. The document observed that before Mary married Bothwell he had been acquitted of Darnley's murder by due process of law, so that she had not entered into the marriage in the knowledge that he had murdered her previous husband, and that the marriage to Bothwell, far from taking place in defiance of public opinion, had been recommended by a large number of lords. It was recalled that at Carberry Mary had surrendered on the promise that she would again have the obedience of her subjects if she abandoned Bothwell, and it was alleged that, after she was separated from Bothwell, no serious attempt was made to apprehend him. Mary's abdication, it was added, had been made under threat of execution. And the final point was made that not a tenth of the nobility had taken part in the coronation of King James. This constituted an able defence against all the charges which Moray had so far brought forward. Admittedly, it was arguable that Bothwell's acquittal, while in accordance with legal procedure, was not in accordance with justice, and it could well be disputed whether the lords who had advised Mary to marry Bothwell were free agents. Nevertheless, all that was said in this 'replication', with the possible exception that insufficient efforts had been made to apprehend Bothwell, were perfectly true. It is not difficult to see why Sussex thought that Mary's 'proofs will fall out best', and it may well have seemed at this stage that the prosecution of Mary, if it was a prosecution, might fail.

On the 20th and 21st the primary business of the enquiry was neglected in favour of a discussion on the rights and wrongs of Moray's regency. This topic was only indirectly relevant, and it was perhaps bad tactics for Mary's commissioners to enter into a discussion of it, since their case postulated that there was no need for a regency at all. On the other hand, a qualified or conditional restoration of Mary might well involve a continuance of a regency, and it did not require any lobbying from the Hamiltons to demonstrate that Moray was never likely to command universal allegiance. At any rate, Mary's commissioners argued that according to the law and practice of Scotland the government during a minority pertained to the nearest in blood, which of course meant the head of the house of Hamilton, who would therefore never acquiesce in Moray's rule. Lord Herries, in conversation, elaborated the point that the heir presumptive had the right by law to be the governor during a minority, and pursued the matter beyond the interest of the immediate circle of Châtelherault and his family. He pointed out that next in the line of succession after them came the Earl of Huntly's family, and then the Earl of Argyll's family, through marriage with daughters of the house of Hamilton, and that they also were resolute against Moray and would stand by the Hamiltons.

These arguments were countered by the contention of Moray's commissioners that according to precedent it was proper for parliament to select a governor to act during a minority. Moray stated that for over five hundred years the practice in Scotland had been for the estates to choose the governor and that the heir presumptive had no prescriptive right. It would appear that, if he himself did not take the Hamilton claim seriously, he feared that Elizabeth might do so. The Earl of Sussex remarked in his letter of 22 October, 'Neither will Moray like of any order whereby he should not be Regent styled; nor Hamilton of any order whereby he should not be as great, or greater, in government than Moray.' Sussex was aware of the argument that King James's heir presumptive was Darnley's brother, Charles, to the exclusion of the Hamiltons. There was, however, some uncertainty, and James MacGill, the Clerk Register, who, as the custodian of the Scottish records, should have been able to speak with authority, told Sussex that, as the King's right to the throne came from his mother it must return 'to the mother's side, which was Hamilton'. But, MacGill significantly added, 'it would put men on horseback before it was performed'.

Both disappointment and anxiety in Moray's mind at this stage are reflected in his urgent demand on the 21st that the proceedings should be hurried on. He was alarmed about what his mission to England was going to cost, especially as Elizabeth was now suggesting that some representatives of the two Scottish parties should go up from York to London. But he also feared the political consequences in Scotland of his prolonged absence, and, of course, if it was common knowledge that the rights and wrongs of his regency were being debated at York it would do nothing to strengthen his position at home.

It may be doubted whether conclusions in such a 'great matter' could ever have been reached at York, without at any rate constant reference to the English court, and it was obvious that progress, and, even more, decision, depended upon Elizabeth and her ministers rather than on anything the English commissioners at York could do. As early as 16 October, when Elizabeth can hardly have thought that the representatives assembled at York had had time to achieve much, she was thinking if not of actually transferring the formal proceedings to her capital, at least of calling to her presence representatives of the parties 'for our own information and more speedy ending of the matters'. She therefore suggested to Norfolk that Sadler should come to London from the English commission, with Lethington and MacGill to represent Moray and Herries to represent Mary, while the Commendator of Kilwinning should be asked 'privately' and 'in a friendly manner' to appear on behalf of Châtelherault. The impression was to be given that the aim of the conversations was Mary's restoration, though with a guarantee of security for the prince and his supporters. This suggestion reached York on the 19th. Moray was able at once to agree to send Lethington and MacGill, but Mary's commissioners had first to consult their mistress. When she heard from them, she welcomed the prospect that her cause was going to be heard by Elizabeth in person, but Knollys had to dampen her optimism by telling her that Elizabeth's purpose was merely 'to be resolved of some doubts' without the delay and expense of 'sending to and fro'. After some discussion, it was agreed that Lesley, Herries and Kilwinning should all go, and Mary gave to Lesley and Herries both an official letter and a personal letter to Elizabeth. On the 22nd the representatives of Moray and Mary set off for the south.

Relieved from the need to attend at York, where nothing was now happening, Moray went sightseeing as far as Hull, while Norfolk paid a visit to Carlisle. Meantime there were rumours of a plot by Lord John Hamilton, son of Châtelherault, to rescue Mary – a useful reminder of the Hamilton interest in the whole business – and Knollys was much concerned about the risk of her escaping.

On 30 October a council at Hampton Court decided that, in future proceedings as in the past, Mary's party should be heard first. Lesley and Herries were therefore to have access to Elizabeth before Moray's representatives, and were to be told in general terms that Elizabeth desired 'some good end'. It was feared that, if they were confronted with the murder charge, they would say that they had no commission beyond the matters contained in Mary's original complaint, and they were therefore to be required to admit to having a general authority to answer all charges. After this, MacGill and Lethington were to be heard, and were to be pressed to bring in the charge of murder. They were to be told that if they did so Elizabeth would protect them from possible vengeance and would never allow Mary to be restored except on conditions agreeable to them. The implication of these decisions by the council was that the hearing was now going to take place in London, and on 3 November Elizabeth intimated to Norfolk that proceedings would be transferred from York.

5. The Enquiry:
The Proceedings at Westminster

The transference of the enquiry from York to Westminster meant a change of setting in more than a physical sense. For one thing, while Mary perhaps thought it an advantage that her commissioners were to be received by Elizabeth and that the latter would presumably have a closer direction over subsequent proceedings, it was to Mary's disadvantage that she herself was further from the scene of the enquiry and that no steps were taken now to bring her to a place 'fifty or sixty miles from London', as had been proposed earlier. Moreover, it was distinctly less promising for Mary that, while she was now further from the scene, yet when Moray, who was in effect her chief antagonist, arrived in London, about 13 November, he was received by Elizabeth in person; this was an inequitable action against which Mary and her commissioners never ceased to protest. On the whole, the indications were increasing that English opinion against Mary was hardening. The fact that her case had made quite a good showing at York undoubtedly suggested to her enemies that stronger action must be taken against her, and Elizabeth's attitude was now distinctly less friendly, partly because of the dangers revealed by the Norfolk marriage project.

Whatever the precise design of the English government, no effort was going to be spared to make the fresh round of proceedings impressive. Possibly one element in the arrangements now made was to ensure that, while the evidence of Mary's guilt was not going to be published to the world, it was going to be disseminated among the most influential men in England, so that they would all know the worst of the woman whom some Englishmen wanted to substitute for Elizabeth. Before the middle of November it was rumoured that Elizabeth meant to assemble not only her privy council, but also most of the earls, to determine 'this great cause', and there was a good deal of truth in this. The new English commission, dated 24 November, named Sir Nicholas Bacon (Keeper of the Great Seal), the Earls of Arundel and Leicester, Lord Clinton and Saye (Lord High Admiral) and Sir William Cecil, the Secretary, as well as Norfolk, Sussex and Sadler, who had been at York, as commissioners to treat with the commissioners of Moray and Mary. Not only so, but when proceedings started these commissioners were joined by the Marquis of Northampton, the Earls of Pembroke, Essex and Bedford and Sir Walter Mildmay. Thus, besides England's solitary duke, there were one of the two marquises and a third of the earls. The commission had spoken of a meeting at 'Westminster or elsewhere', but it had already been decided that Westminster should be the place. This choice seemed objectionable to Mary's commissioners and also to the Duke of Châtelherault, who on 23 November, at Hampton Court, protested against it, on the ground that 'that place is judicial, where causes civil and criminal use to be treated'. Elizabeth, however, explained afresh that she was not going to act as a judge and that the chamber selected at Westminster was not a place where judgements were given.

Considerably more state attended the new setting of the enquiry, and the proceedings are more fully and more formally reported than those at York had been. It was on Thursday, 25 November, that the hearing opened, in the Painted Chamber, described as 'next on the north to the parliament chamber at Westminster'. One of Elizabeth's commissioners, the Earl of Arundel, was unable to attend by reason of sickness and was not sworn in until 1 December, but the other seven, seated at 'a long table, being a table of council', produced their commission under Elizabeth's seal, in green wax, and read it to Lesley, Boyd, Herries and Kilwinning, as commissioners appointed by Mary under her signature and signet on 29 September. The English commissioners announced that they did not mean to proceed judicially, but this did not obviate a renewal of the protest by Mary's commissioners that they could not submit to judgement, since Mary was a sovereign princess, and they withdrew into 'an inner little chamber'. Then Moray, Morton, Adam Bothwell, Dunfermline and Lindsay, commissioners for Mary's son, 'entitled by them James, King of Scotland', entered the great chamber and read their commission, under the great seal of Scotland, in yellow wax. Mary's commissioners then returned and the oaths and protests made at York were repeated by all three parties on the New Testament, held to them by Humphrey Parkins, canon of Westminster, who is described rather oddly as 'chief prebendary of the cathedral church of Westminster', although Westminster Abbey had been a cathedral only from 1540 to 1550 and had become a collegiate church after Elizabeth's accession.

It was on 26 November, the second day of the conference, that Moray at length received an answer to the four 'articles' or questions which he had posed at York on 9 October. The answer had been long in the making because of the obvious difficulties the questions presented. On 30 October Cecil had drafted an answer in extremely cautious phraseology. The English government, he argued, thought the questions needed no particular answer, but a general assurance could be given that Elizabeth, on the termination of the hearing of the cause, would maintain the innocent and reprove the guilty. With such an assurance the Queen hoped Moray would be content, but should he persist in his request and should she give a more precise answer, he was not to be encouraged thereby to enter into accusations of Mary for any crime, since Elizabeth's principal wish was that upon the hearing of 'this great cause' the honour and estate of the Queen of Scots should be preserved and found 'sound, whole and firm'. Such an answer, had it been publicised, would have been something much less decisive than Moray had hoped for, and far more satisfactory to Mary than to him. If such was the English view it justified Mary's confidence and Moray's anxiety. Indeed, it may be suspected that this draft was scrapped after the English council, on the same day, decided that Moray's party should be pressed to bring in the murder charge. Consequently, the answer which Moray actually received on 26 November proceeded to definite answers to his four questions: (1) The English commissioners had full powers in terms of their commission. (2) They would report to their Queen what they found to be true, and Elizabeth would then, without unnecessary delay, pronounce what appeared to her to be true. (3) Should Mary be found guilty, 'which were much to be lamented', she would either be delivered to Moray on security for the safety of her life and for good usage of her person, or else would continue in England at the expense of the Scottish government, in such a way that neither Moray, James, nor any other would be in danger from her. (4) Besides, should Mary be found guilty, Elizabeth would approve of Moray's proceedings and recognise his authority until it might be proved that some other person should be governor or some other form of government should be adopted.

Thus fortified, Moray and his colleagues could no longer refuse to proceed with their further accusations, and on the same day, after protesting that they proceeded to accuse Mary of murder only under necessity and unwillingly, they produced their 'Eik',

7

or addition to their former answer. The Scottish courtier, Sir James Melville, in his lively *Memoirs*, has a picturesque account of the production of the 'Eik' which, though not supported by the official account of the proceedings, is not seriously at variance with them. Melville suggests that Moray had not even yet received all he wanted, namely a guarantee in writing under Elizabeth's seal, and that he was still disposed to withhold his 'Eik', but that his continued reluctance to produce it was frustrated by the action of Adam Bothwell, Bishop of Orkney. The Bishop, as it happened, had won some renown for his agility on an earlier occasion. In 1567, when he went with Kirkaldy of Grange in pursuit of the Earl of Bothwell after Carberry, they almost overtook Bothwell's ships in the north entrance to Bressay Sound, in Shetland, but the Earl's pilot steered close to a hidden rock and Kirkaldy's ship, pressing on in the chase, ran aground. The incident was related in a vivid manner by Mark Napier in his *Memoirs of Merchiston*, and his acount deserves to be reprinted as an example of Victorian historiography at its most spirited.

'It was not long before two vessels were descried cruising off the east coast of Shetland, where currents, tides and whirlpools threatened destruction to the most skilful navigator. These vessels were the Duke of Orkney's [Bothwell's], on the look out, and manned by desperate seamen. Grange, who commanded the swiftest of the government ships, shot ahead, and approached Bressay Sound, through which the pirates steered. Onward pressed their pursuers, and every nerve was strained on board the *Unicorn*, Grange's ship, to gain their object. The manoeuvre of the fugitives would have done credit to the more practised days of the Red Rover. So close was the chase, that, when the pirate escaped by the north passage of the sound, Grange came in by the south, and continued the chase northward. But the fugitives were familiar with those narrow and dangerous seas. They knew how lightly their own vessels could dash through the boiling eddy that betrayed a sunken rock, and discerned at a glance what would be the fate of their bulky pursuers if they dared to follow in their desperate track. They steered accordingly upon breakers; and though the keel grazed the rocks, their vessel glided through the cresting foam, and shot into a safer sea. Grange ordered every sail to be set to impel the *Unicorn* in the very same path. In vain his more experienced mariners remonstrated. The warlike baron, as if leading a charge of horse in the plains of Flanders, rushed on the breakers, and instantly his gallant ship was a wreck – there being just time to hoist out a boat and save the ship's company and soldiers. As it was, one warrior heavily armed still clung to the wreck, and, the boat being already on its way deeply laden, it seemed impossible to save this being from destruction. His cries reached them, but were disregarded; another instant of delay and he had perished, when, collecting all his energies, he sprung with a desperate effort into the midst of the crowded boat, causing it to reel with his additional weight, encumbered as he was with a corslet of proof; "which," says Godscroft, who records the incident, "was thought a strange leap, especially not to have overturned the boat." Who would have surmised that this athletic man-at-arms, the last to quit the wreck, was a bishop! – the bishop who had so lately joined the hand of him he pursued, with that of Queen Mary! – the very bishop who a month before had poured the holy oil in the infant head of James VI and stood proxy for the extorted abdication of that monarch's mother. It was Adam Bothwell, Bishop of Orkney. The rock from which he leapt can be seen at low water, and is called the Unicorn to this day.'

This spectacular leap had not been forgotten when the Bishop appeared, in a very different rôle, at Westminster. Sir James Melville relates that when Norfolk asked Moray for the 'Eik', the Regent

'desired again the assurance of the conviction [of Mary] by writing and seal, as is said. It was answered again that the Queen's Majesty's word, being a true princess, was sufficient. Then all the council cried out, "Would he mistrust the Queen, who had given such proof of her friendship to Scotland?" The Regent's council cried out also in that same manner. Then Secretary Cecil asked if they had the accusation there. "Yes," says Mr John Wood; and with that he plucks it out of his bosom, "But I will not deliver it till Her Majesty's hand-writ and seal be delivered to my Lord Regent for what he demands." Then the Bishop of Orkney snatcheth the writ out of Mr John Wood's hand. "Let me have it," says he, "I shall present it." Mr John ran after him, as if he would have it again or torn his clothes. Forward goes the bishop to the council table, and gives in the accusation. Then said to him my Lord William Howard, chamberlain of England, "Well done, Bishop Turpy; thou art the smartest fellow among them all; none of them will make thy leap good;" scorning him for his leaping out of the laird of

Grange's ship ... The Regent ... desired the accusation to be rendered up to him again, alleging that he had some more to add thereto. They answered that they would hold what they had, and were ready to receive any other addition when he should please to give it in. The Duke of Norfolk had enough ado to keep his countenance. Mr John Wood winked upon Secretary Cecil, who smiled again upon him.'

It has been suggested, and Melville's account might almost be taken to imply as much, that the incident was stage-managed, to give Moray an excuse for claiming that his hand had been forced. It might be that his associates had lost patience with his extreme caution and were determined to delay no longer, but it would be quite in character with Moray's habitual skill in covering his tracks if he sought a pretext for shifting on to others the responsibility for decisive action. Elizabeth, who, nearly twenty years later, was to follow a similar course by placing on her secretary the responsibility for despatching Mary's death-warrant, must surely have found in Moray a congenial ally.

The text of the 'Eik', signed by Moray and his fellow commissioners, is as follows:

'An Eik to the answer presented by us, James, Earl of Moray and Regent ... and remaining commissioners ... to the letter presented to your grace and the lords commissioners for the Queen's Majesty of England....

'Whereas in our former answer, upon good respects mentioned in our protestation, we kept back the chiefest causes and grounds whereupon our actions and whole proceedings were founded, wherewithall seeing our adversaries will not content themselves, but by their obstinate and earnest pressing we are compelled for justifying of our cause to manifest the naked truth: it is certain, as we boldly and constantly affirm, that, as James, sometime Earl of Bothwell, was the chief executor of the horrible and unworthy murder perpetrated in the person of the deceased King Henry of good memory, father of our sovereign lord and the Queen's lawful husband, so was she of the foreknowledge, counsel, device, persuader and commander of the said murder to be done, maintainer and fortifier of the executors thereof, by impending and stopping of the inquisition and punishment due for the same according to the laws of the realm, and, consequently, by marriage with the same James, sometime Earl Bothwell, delated and universally esteemed chief author of the abovenamed murder. Wherethrough they began to use and exercise an uncouth and cruel tyranny in the whole state of the commonwealth and with the first (as well appeared by their proceedings) intended to cause the innocent prince, now our sovereign lord, shortly follow his father, and so to transfer the crown from the right line to a bloody murderer and godless tyrant. In which respect the estates of the realm of Scotland, finding her unworthy to reign, decerned her demission of the crown, with the coronation of our sovereign lord and establishing of the regiment of the realm in the person of me, the Earl of Moray, during His Highness's minority, to be lawfully, sufficiently and righteously done, as in the acts and laws made thereupon more largely is contained.'

After a busy and perhaps exciting day on Friday, 26 November, when this decisive step had been taken, the commissioners went off on Saturday to spend the weekend at Hampton Court, where they saw Elizabeth but apparently transacted no business. On Monday the 29th they were back in London, where the next step was for Elizabeth's commissioners to ask Moray and his colleagues whether they wished the 'Eik' to be delivered to Mary's representatives. They gave their assent to this, and in the afternoon a copy of the 'Eik' was handed to Lesley and his colleagues. After withdrawing for a time, they returned to declare that they found it strange that the other party should put such matter into writing, especially considering that Mary had been generous to so many of them. They declared their readiness to defend their mistress, but asked for time to consider their answer in a matter of such weight and offered to return after noon the next day. It turned out that they had not allowed themselves enough time, for on the 30th, 'about twelve of the clock at dinner time', they sent a messenger asking for further deferment until 9 a.m. the following day.

On Wednesday, 1 December, Mary's commissioners entered and sat down at the council table, now ready with their reply to the 'Eik', in the shape of a counter-accusation of Moray and his party. Herries acted as spokesman, and made the following statement:

'The Queen's Highness, our and their native sovereign, being of herself (as well is known) a liberal princess, gave them in her youth for their unshamefaced begging, without other their worthy deservings, the two part of the patrimony pertaining to the crown of Scotland. And when her grace came to further years and more perfect understanding, they, seeing that her successors, kings of that realm, might not maintain their estate upon the third part (albeit her grace might for the time, having so great a dowry in France and other casualties apart from the property of the crown), procured her slander so far as in them was, besides slaying her secretary in her presence. They were aware that she could use the privilege of the laws, always granted to the kings of that realm of before, and make revocation before her full age of twenty-five years, and understood right well that this was a way, when it pleased her grace or her successors, by the laws of the realm, to take from them the livings before giving them. When they had herein advised with their Machiavelli's doctrine, and seeing her son an infant not a year old, they could find no better way than to cut off their sovereign liege lady (which, if it had not been for the great diligence of the Queen's Majesty of this realm, without doubt had been done) – for that they understood they might long possess those rooms* before that infant had wit or power to displace them, and in the meantime get great riches under the colour of a pretended authority. That it was not the punishment of the slaughter of Darnley that moved them to this proud rebellion, but the usurping of their sovereign's authority and to possess themselves with her great riches and her true subjects, we will boldly avow and constantly affirm the same to be, as by the sequels doth and shall plainly appear.'

It may seem altogether too simple, if not naïve, to represent the course of Mary's relations with her lords as nothing more than the outcome of a dispute about property, but the point which Herries made about the matter of a revocation is certainly significant. Any student of the period who is familiar also with the general course of Scottish history must wonder if it was only a coincidence that the rebellion against Mary occurred when she was in her twenty-fifth year, which she entered in December 1566, for it was in his twenty-fifth year that a Scottish sovereign was accustomed to make a revocation of grants made during his minority. Such a revocation had always been dreaded by acquisitive nobles who had been making inroads on crown property. A revocation had something to do with the troubles which brought James V's reign to its disastrous close, and exactly a century later a revocation had a great deal to do with the unrest which led to the downfall of Charles I. Did the fear of a revocation lie behind Mary's troubles in 1567 and were the acquisitive nobles determined to get rid of her before she could execute a revocation in her fatal twenty-fifth year? A hint

* I.e., possessions, in the sense of holdings of land.

that this was so is given by Sir James Melville in his *Memoirs*, and the contention that the fear of a revocation was the real motive of the rebels of 1567 did not make its first appearance with the defence against Moray's 'Eik' at Westminster. Mary, in her first interview with Knollys and Scrope when she arrived in England, had said that the real cause of the rebellion was the desire of the rebels 'to keep by violence that which she had so liberally given them, since by her revocation thereof within full age [i.e., before she was twenty-five] they could not enjoy it by law'. Evidently Mary's allegation reached Scotland and was taken seriously there, for there is a paper, endorsed by Cecil with the date 5 June, in the hand of John Wood, Moray's secretary, repudiating the charge. Mary alluded much later to the revocation she would have made if she had not been prevented by the revolution of 1567.

After the statement which has been quoted, Herries invited Elizabeth's commissioners to consider how dangerous an example it was for subjects to bring in false accusations against their sovereign, and said that on investigation it would appear that some of those who were now accusing Mary were themselves privy to the making of bonds for the death of Darnley. Lesley then made a speech concerned rather with the future procedure of the enquiry. He said that Mary's commissioners could go no further until they had additional instructions from her, for she had told them that, if the other party brought up matters not raised at York, they should not answer them. He introduced a new element into the discussions by asking that Mary should be allowed to appear in person and answer for her own defence in presence of Elizabeth, the council and nobility of England and such ambassadors of foreign princes as happened to be in the country, and that in the meantime the other party might be 'arrested and stayed' until a conclusion on his proposal was reached. He produced letters signed by Mary on 22 November supporting what he had just said and the request he had made.

On Thursday, 2 December, Lesley resumed his attack, protesting that although Elizabeth had refused to receive Mary she had received Moray, and repeating that he and his fellows were resolved to make a request to Elizabeth that Mary should be allowed to appear personally before her. Some of the English commissioners then went to Hampton Court to consult their Queen and returned to intimate that Mary's commissioners should attend at Hampton Court on Friday the 3rd. The latter, accordingly, presented their supplication on Friday to Elizabeth, who promised an answer next day.

Before giving her answer on the 4th Elizabeth met her own commissioners and her privy council. She explained that she would not receive Mary as long as she was defamed by accusations, and, while she thought it reasonable that Mary should have a hearing, she had not determined in what way this should be done. Early in the afternoon, Lesley and his associates asked Leicester and Cecil to speak with them 'apart' before they went to receive the Queen's answer. In the Earl's room, they explained that they were forbidden to answer the accusations and were empowered only to request, as they had done the previous day, that Mary might appear in person. Lesley said, however, that they were prepared to assist in an enquiry with a view to a settlement which would give security to Moray and his party, and they wanted Elizabeth to be informed of this and to be asked if she would agree to such a plan. If she would neither agree to some compromise nor allow Mary to appear in person, they could proceed no further in the conference. Herries also spoke, in support of Lesley. Leicester and Cecil thought that there was some obscurity in the point of view which the Scotsmen were trying to put forward, and asked for a statement in writing, but they obtained only some notes in which other matter was intermingled.

When Herries and Lesley, after their private talk with Leicester and Cecil, came into Elizabeth's presence, she asked them to repeat their 'motion'. After they had done so, she reiterated her desire to have the cause well ended and Mary freed from suspicion, and added that, despite their 'motion of appointment', she could not forget her office as a friend and a sister. She said she had therefore thought it better that Moray and his accomplices should be charged, and then reproved and punished for defaming their Queen, rather than that the matter should be ended by 'appointment' – unless, that is, Moray could prove his case. As for Mary's appearance in person, she could not be brought to answer, as it were, in her defence, before a tribunal, unless Moray's accusation 'might first appear to have more likelihood of just cause than she did find therein, for she rather hoped that the same should be found to be devised without just ground. And, so finding it, the Queen's honour should be thereby saved, without either any composition by appointment or any necessity for answer.'

Herries and Lesley explained that the motion for an 'appointment' had not come from Mary after the accusation of murder had been given in, but had been made on their own initiative, partly because of their own desire to have 'things quietly ended' and partly on the strength of Mary's earlier 'disposition' that the whole cause should be ended by 'appointment'. However, Elizabeth still did not approve of the proposal. They therefore went on to renew their request for Mary's personal appearance. On this too she was adamant, though she repeated that she hoped to 'reprehend and impugn' the accusation, in Mary's interest.

The attitude of Mary's representatives at this point surely suggests that they were finding a defence difficult. Mary herself was still looking for a triumphant conclusion in her own favour, and it is significant that it was not she, but her commissioners, who proposed a compromise at this point. It seems that her commissioners did not share her confidence and rather feared the results of an investigation of the charges. Whether Elizabeth's words expressed her real intent it is hard to say. If she wanted Moray's charges pressed, it is more likely to have been because she saw them leading to the damning of Mary's reputation rather than, as she said, because she hoped for Mary's informal acquittal.

A Sunday again intervened before the conference resumed on Monday, 6 December. The English commissioners gathered in the early afternoon in the accustomed chamber in order to declare to Moray and his associates Elizabeth's professed dislike of their late accusation of Mary. The Regent and his fellows had been summoned to attend for this purpose, but, before they appeared, Mary's commissioners asked if they might be heard again, and the English commissioners agreed to see them before Moray's party was admitted. Mary's representatives then related that, since they had learned on Saturday that Elizabeth was going to hear the proofs of Moray's allegations before hearing Mary, they had now come to protest that, unless Mary could appear in person before Elizabeth, the conference should be dissolved. The English commissioners, however, took the view that Mary's men were representing Elizabeth's statement 'otherwise than was both plainly and manifestly known' to the Englishmen who had been present at Hampton Court when Elizabeth had made it, and that the protest could therefore not be accepted. Lesley and his colleagues then retired.

Moray and his party now entered. The Lord Keeper told them that Elizabeth thought it very strange that they, 'being native subjects to the Queen of Scots, should accuse her of so horrible a crime', and added: 'Although you in thus doing have forgotten your duties of allegiance towards her, your sovereign, yet her Majesty means not to forget the office of a good sister and of a good neighbour and friend. What you are to answer to this, we are here ready to hear.' Moray's party recalled that they had originally gone to York to answer accusations by Mary, and they thought at first that they had given a good enough justification of their doings without accusing the Queen. But, when their adversaries had in their 'replication' made so many charges of disobedience, they had been obliged to retaliate. They said they had prepared for production a 'collection made in writing of the presumptions and circumstances by the which it should evidently appear that as the Earl of Bothwell was the chief murderer of the King, so was the Queen a deviser and maintainer thereof'. Along with this 'collection' Moray brought forward, as evidence that the three estates of Scotland had ratified and approved his party's proceedings as lawful, an act of parliament of December 1567.

The 'collection of presumptions and circumstances' which appeared at this point was in fact the Book of Articles, a full-scale indictment of Mary, which is printed in full and critically examined in detail in chapter 6. There is no doubt that this document had a long and involved pedigree, going back at least to the summer of 1568, when the possibility had emerged of an investigation at which the case against Mary would be examined, but quite likely to a point more than a year earlier, when the confederate lords must have considered the grounds on which they could justify their revolution against criticisms from England and perhaps elsewhere. Among its antecedents were the first draft of George Buchanan's *Detectio Mariae Reginae Scotorum*, a rough translation by Buchanan of that same *Detectio* in the form of an 'Indictment', and a 'Narrative' prepared by the Earl of Lennox. These documents, the Book of Articles itself, the Casket Letters and the works subsequently published by Buchanan, culminating in his *History* (1582), contain a number of discrepancies which suggest a startling disregard for consistency and indeed for truth. The question has been raised whether the Book of Articles as it survives is precisely the document which was produced at Westminster in December 1568, but any differences are unlikely to have been substantial, and the same general criticism can be applied to it as has been applied to Buchanan's *History* by its latest editor: 'Buchanan had before him a sequence of events of undeniable authenticity, while there was available to him a great deal of circumstantial evidence which could have been used against the Queen with much effect; but instead of relying upon irrefutable evidence he saw fit to build his indictment on allegations and insinuations which are demonstrably suspect.'

Before the meeting of 6 December closed, the Book of Articles had been read to the English commission. Next day, when the

English commission reassembled at 9 a.m., three chapters of the Book of Articles were read over anew, along with 'the two other papers' [i.e., the acts of privy council and parliament of December 1567].* Moray and his colleagues then came in, by appointment, and said that after the English commissioners had read the Book of Articles and seen the act of parliament they would surely think the Regent's party innocent of crime and would be satisfied of their 'good meaning' at York. Proofs of any of the Articles were offered, but the commissioners said that, as they were not judges, they could not require anything more than each party chose to utter. However, Moray and his party, after withdrawing for a time, returned with the Casket and a selection from its contents.

Next day, the 8th, Moray and his colleagues produced seven additional items from the Casket, saying they were letters written by the Queen, and handed over copies of them. They also brought forward a further collection of material of a more assorted kind. The principal items in this collection were the proceedings in the trials of Hay, Hepburn, Powrie and Dalgleish, the retainers of Bothwell who had been executed for their part in the murder of Darnley and whose confessions and depositions, now produced at Westminster, incriminated Bothwell.† Further productions related to Bothwell – the judgement of parliament against him and Mary's remission to him. Finally, there was the 'Protestation' of Huntly and Argyll.‡

It is surely somewhat remarkable, to say the least, that Moray proceeded to his full-scale indictment, in the Book of Articles, only after Mary's representatives had declined to take any further part in the proceedings. It is perhaps even more remarkable that the Casket Letters were likewise publicly produced only when there was no one at Westminster to challenge them. Indeed, of those who were said to have been present at the opening of the Casket on 21 June 1567, only Morton and Lethington were at Westminster, and only they could have known whether the contents had been tampered with. Short of an examination of the originals, the evidence for the authenticity of the documents rested on the testimony of those two alone. Here, of course, we see the consequences of the peculiar character of the investigation. Because the proceedings were not strictly judicial, not those of a court of law, the evidence was not subjected to cross-examination, as it would have been in normal legal process. Equally, no witnesses

* See p. 57 above.
† See p. 46 above.
‡ See pp. 29–30 above.

were called. Moray did produce the written depositions of a number of witnesses against Bothwell, but even those appeared only at the same late stage as the Casket Letters and were never open to challenge on Mary's behalf. Not only so, but the witnesses themselves, far from being available for cross-examination, were already dead.

On the morning of Thursday, 9 December, Elizabeth's commissioners were still occupied with the Casket; they were 'perusing certain letters and sonnets written in French and duly translated into English', with other writings also exhibited to them by Moray. While they were so engaged, Lesley and Boyd sent a messenger to ask for a hearing, which was granted to them for 'one of the clock after dinner'; and a similar request from Moray was met by giving him an appointment for 2 p.m. Until dinner time the commissioners continued their hearing and reading of 'the said writings'. Lesley and Boyd arrived an hour later, at two o'clock, with a protestation signed by them and also by Herries and Kilwinning. It was a modified version of their protestation of the 6th, which had not been received because it was held to have misrepresented Elizabeth's meaning. This new version recited the refusal of Mary's commissioners to give an answer to the 'Eik', declared that Mary would answer only in Elizabeth's presence, and recalled the supplication presented to Elizabeth at Hampton Court on the 3rd that Mary be permitted to answer in person. Mary's commissioners now claimed that, as that earlier supplication had not been directly answered by Elizabeth at their audience on the 4th, the proceedings must now be considered to be at an end. They withdrew, and Moray and his party were next received. Morton produced a written statement about the discovery of the Casket and took his oath as to its truth. Further evidence was brought forward in the shape of statements by Thomas Nelson, the servant of Darnley who had escaped the death at Kirk o' Field, and Thomas Crawford, a servant of the Earl of Lennox, as well as the act of parliament of 15 December 1567 which narrated Mary's demission of the crown.

On 10 December the only significant proceeding was the composition of Moray's party of a testimony to the authenticity of the documents they had produced: 'For verification of the Eik or addition to our answer . . . concerning the murder of the late King Henry . . . we have produced divers missive letters, sonnets, obligations or contracts for marriage . . . We . . . testify . . . that the said . . . writings . . . are undoubtedly the said Queen's proper handwrit, except the contract in Scots of the date at Seton

5 April 1567, written by the Earl of Huntly, which also we understand and perfectly know to be subscribed by her.' Needless to say, this went unchallenged, for there was no one present to challenge it.

6. The Book of Articles:
The Accusations Examined

THE BOOK OF ARTICLES,
OR COMPREHENSIVE INDICTMENT OF MARY,
PRESENTED BY THE EARL OF MORAY AT WESTMINSTER,
IS HERE REPRINTED IN MODERNISED SPELLING
AND TERMINOLOGY, AND ITS
ACCURACY EXAMINED CLAUSE
BY CLAUSE.

Articles containing certain conjectures, presumptions, likelihoods and circumstances by the which it shall evidently appear that, as James, sometime Earl Bothwell, was the chief executor of the horrible and unworthy murder perpetrated in the person of the deceased King Henry of good memory, father to our said sovereign lord and the Queen's lawful husband, so was she of the foreknowledge, counsel, devise, persuader and commander of the said murder to be done, and maintainer, fortifier of the executors thereof: divided in five parts.

The first part contains the alteration of the said Queen's affection from the deceased King Henry, our sovereign lord's father, her lawful husband of good memory, in converting her ardent love towards him in extreme disdain and deadly hatred.

The second part contains the said Queen's inordinate affection borne to James, sometime Earl Bothwell, in the lifetime of the King, her husband, yea both before and after his murder.

The third part contains the conspiracy, device and execution of the said deceased King Henry's horrible murder by the said Queen, his wife, and Bothwell.

The fourth part contains the sequel of the said murder from the committing thereof to the accomplishing of the pretended and unlawful marriage between the said Queen and Bothwell.

The fifth and last part contains how, by occasion of the punishment of the said murder neglected, the noblemen and other good subjects took arms and detained and sequestrated the said Queen's person for a time, and of their proceedings thereafter.

THE FIRST PART,
CONTAINING THE ALTERATION OF
THE QUEEN'S MIND AND AFFECTION FROM
THE DECEASED KING, OUR SOVEREIGN LORD'S FATHER,
HER LAWFUL HUSBAND, BY CONVERTING HER
ARDENT LOVE TOWARDS HIM IN
EXTREME DISDAIN IN
DEADLY HATRED.

After her vehement love borne towards the King, whereupon followed the marriage solemnised between them the 29 day of July 1565, she suddenly altered the same about November next thereafter, for she removed and secluded him from the council and knowledge of all council affairs, whereby it appeared the love lasted not above three months between them.

About the beginning of January in the same year [1565–6] a new coinage of silver was devised to be set forth, whereon both their faces were ordained to be imprinted, and in the circumscription his name preferred, as it was in all letters and patents continually after their marriage and until his death, yet in evident token of her disdain towards him she caused the form of that coinage be suddenly altered and in the circumscription placed first her own name, as *Maria et Henricus Dei gratia Regina et Rex Scotorum*, contrary to the order of nature and observance of all princes in the like case.

The Register of the Privy Council, so far as it is extant, is inadequate in itself to substantiate the allegation that Darnley was suddenly excluded from the council, for it does not show that either Darnley or Mary was a frequent attender. Darnley was present (with Mary) on 12 September and 10 October 1565, but Mary herself is rarely named as being present alone either before or after those dates.

On 22 December 1565 a proclamation running, as usual, in the names of 'The King and Queen's Majesties' is followed by an act in the names of 'Our Sovereigns Queen's and King's Majesties' ordering the issue of new coins, with the inscription: 'Maria et Henricus Dei gratia Regina et Rex Scotorum'. However, the proclamation immediately following again runs 'Henry and

*Mary . . .' Besides, all documents issued under the great and privy
seals continued to run in the names of King Henry and Queen
Mary until Darnley's death.*

*So far as the Register of the Privy Council shows, the exclusion
of Darnley from public business did not take place until much later
than the Book of Articles suggests. Only after the winter of 1565–6
did Mary take the main burden of state business upon herself. In
September 1566 a petition was said to be presented to 'the Queen's
majesty and lords of Secret Council'; acts of council passed at
Jedburgh in October 1566 made no mention of the King, but as
soon as the council was back in Edinburgh his name reappears,
before the Queen's; and it is only from 20 December 1566 (when
there is an act superscribed 'Regina' and signed by the Queen
alone) that Darnley's name finally disappears.*

Continuing in her disdain she determined to seclude him from
all knowledge of the public affairs and to the end that by subscribing with her (to which honour she wilfully accepted him) he
should not understand what letters passed, she caused make a
printing iron and used the same in all things in place of his subscription.

Of all the noblemen then exiled she granted remission only to
the Duke of Châtelherault, known enemy to the King, her husband,
his father and the whole house, in his and their despite. And,
knowing the King had opposed him thereto if he had been made
privy to the same, she caused sign the remission with the printing
iron as the King's subscription, utterly refusing the like favour to
the remaining noblemen of her own and the King's surname and
other ancient friends to the house of Lennox, notwithstanding the
King her husband's earnest desire and special requests of the
Queen's majesty of England and King of France, sent to that
effect.

*It may well be that Darnley's absence on his own pleasures, both
before and after his estrangement from his wife, led almost inevitably to his partial seclusion from business. It can be shown
that when both of them signed a document, Mary's signature was
apt to come first, in the same ink as the body of the document,
while Darnley's came second, sometimes in a different ink. This
suggests that he was not always readily available. The convenience
of a 'printing iron' or stamp is not incomprehensible. A passport to
Châtelherault, dated 30 January 1565–6 and bearing the stamped
signature, is in the possession of the Duke of Hamilton at Lennox-
love.*

It is true that Châtelherault had his remission on 2 January

1566, though it was not to him alone but to about a hundred and sixty Hamiltons of varying degree.

Through this her disdain, continued against the King, her husband, not only did she show this special and extraordinary favour to his known enemy, but began to be rigorous and extreme to his friends and kinsmen, namely to the Earl of Morton, chancellor of the realm, from whom she caused the great seal to be taken, the keeping whereof properly belongs to his office, and put the same seal in the custody of others, against the lovable order and custom of the country, he having the office of chancellory and keeping of the great seal for his lifetime and having committed no offence that could be imputed to him.

Morton was so far from 'having committed no offence' that the reason for the revocation of his appointment as chancellor was in truth his part in the murder of Rizzio. The Earl of Huntly was appointed to succeed him on 20 March 1566, eleven days after that event. The Book of Articles is completely silent about the Rizzio murder and its effect on Mary's attitude to Darnley and others.

Although the printing iron of the King's counterfeit subscription was lost, yet, continuing in her disdain, she would not permit the King to subscribe letters and signatures with her, passing in the names of them both, but invents a new device and in place of his subscription wrote *Fiat* after her own name for warrant to the signet and seals, secluding him thereby utterly from the knowledge of the state of the realm.

It should be said that there were sometimes political reasons for issuing documents over Mary's name alone, because the English government did not recognise Darnley as King and refused to accept a safe-conduct which bore his signature. There is evidence of documents in which Mary wrote Fiat after her name.

This her rooted disdain still continuing, a little before her delivery of her birth, in May or June 1566, in making of her latter will and testament, she named and appointed Bothwell among others to the guardianship of her birth and issue and government of the realm in case of her decease, and unnaturally secluded the father from all kind of care and government over his own child, advancing Bothwell above all others to be lieutenant general if wars should happen in the prince's less age. She disponed also her whole movables to others besides her husband. And, lest reason should have overthrown this her latter will among the nobility after her decease, she caused them to give their solemn oath for observance of the whole contents thereof, without inspection of anything contained therein.

The allegation that Bothwell was specially favoured in the arrangements made at this time is hard to reconcile with the fact that when Mary went into Edinburgh Castle for her confinement Argyll and Moray were lodged with her, while Huntly and Bothwell were not. The allegation that 'she disponed also her whole movables to others besides her husband' is contradicted by the evidence of an inventory of Mary's possessions drawn up at this time and annotated by her in the margin to indicate her wishes for their disposal. There are no less than fifteen marginal references to Darnley, and the number of articles destined for him may have been as many as twenty-six. There were only two bequests to Bothwell. It is possible, but extremely improbable, that Mary drew up a will which has not survived and which was completely contrary in its sense to this testamentary inventory. The inventory was edited by Joseph Robertson in Inventaires de la Royne descosse (Bannatyne Club, 1863), 93 ff.

Being delivered of her birth, and thereafter convalesced of her infirmity, the King, her husband, suiting to be admitted to bed with her, was rejected. And she, disdaining him and fleeing his company, suddenly passed out of the castle of Edinburgh by water to Alloa, conducted with certain notorious pirates such as William Blacater, Edmund Blacater, Leonard Robertson, Thomas Dickson and their fellows, avowed men and dependers on Bothwell, to the great wonder of all honest persons, seeing her take the sea without any honest man to accompany her: which William Blacater thereafter was at the murder of the King, her husband, and was put to death for the same.

In Alloa what was the form of her behaviour anew perceived little to their contentment, seeing it more wantonly and honestly and far exceeding the modesty requisite in such a personage. Always the King, her husband, hearing of her sudden departing, quickly followed, and by Stirling came to Alloa, of purpose to attend upon her according to his duty. But at his coming he neither received good countenance nor hearty entertainment of her, and scarcely had reposed him, his servants and horses, with meat, when it behoved him to depart, so great was her disdain that she could not suffer him to remain in her company nor yet would she declare any glad cheer in his presence.

Mary's estrangement from Darnley after the birth of the prince was real enough, as has been explained in chapter 2. However, this account of the visit to Alloa is highly suspect. To travel from

Edinburgh by boat up the Firth of Forth to Alloa at the end of July was quite the most comfortable way for Mary to make the first journey she had undertaken since her confinement. It may be true that William and Edmund Blacater had not unstained records – perhaps few seamen had in those days – for each had had a respite for a murder, and William was in fact executed for his part in Darnley's murder. On the other hand, while William may or may not himself have been a pirate, on 2 September 1566 he was given an official commission to apprehend pirates. Bothwell, as Lord High Admiral, may well have found the crew for the vessel which conveyed the Queen, but it is not at all clear that he himself went to Alloa at all. Besides, at Alloa Mary and her party (which included probably Lethington and possibly Moray) were the guests of the very respectable Earl and Countess of Mar. Darnley undoubtedly visited his wife while she was there and, while he may have been 'disdainfully' received, it is worth noting that shortly afterwards he received from Mary a large cash payment, as well as a quantity of cloth of gold. The Book of Articles omits mention of the closer association of Mary and Darnley in August.

Hereafter, in September 1566, she lodged in the Exchequer House in Edinburgh, and the King, lying at Stirling, thought good to try again if she would accept him to familiarity, which she hearing purposely fled out of the Exchequer House and passed to the palace of Holyroodhouse, where the King coming, he was rejected and rebuked openly in presence of diverse lords then of her privy council, until he was constrained to return to Stirling. By the way, out of Corstorphine, he wrote to her, lamenting his evil treatment and hostile usage.

There are official accounts of the relations of Darnley and Mary in September 1566 which seem more likely to be accurate than the Book of Articles. When Mary left Stirling for the Exchequer in Edinburgh she offered to bring Darnley with her, but he insisted on remaining at Stirling. Lennox, after visiting him, informed Mary that Darnley had a ship ready to take him out of the country. The letter reached Mary on 29 September and Darnley arrived the same day. He at first refused to enter Holyroodhouse, but Mary persuaded him to enter and he passed the night in her room. Next day Darnley met the council, with Du Croc, and was reminded of the 'wise and virtuous' conduct of his wife, while he, on his part, denied that she had given him cause for discontent, but he sulkily withdrew and then told Mary in a letter that he was still thinking of leaving the country, as he was deprived of royal authority and abandoned by the nobles. The council commented that they would never agree to his having the disposal of affairs.

About the middle of October, she lying extremely sick in Jedburgh, the King in haste came from Stirling to visit her, where of her or any other he received neither good words nor good countenance, neither meat, drink nor lodging was prepared or appointed for him. But the Queen in the extremity of her sickness continued in her disdain in such sort that none of the lords or officers there attending dared once look to him or do him reverence and humanity. And especially she, fearing that my lord Earl of Moray, now Regent, should show him that benevolence to give him his chamber, she sent my lord's wife speedily to the chamber, willing her to counterfeit herself to be sick, to the end the King should not suit the lodging, or in case he sought in my Lady Moray's sickness might be a sufficient excuse why he should not have it. So, compelled to borrow the Bishop of Orkney's bed for that night, he returned again to Stirling, being willed, yea and commanded, not to resort to Monsieur le Comte de Biran, the King of France's ambassador, until the time of the baptism, that his apparel might be prepared, fearing he should have disclosed his hard and unnatural treatment. But when all this difficulty was made to get him lodging, meat and drink for a night, she was so careful for Bothwell even in the extremity of her sickness that she caused him be transported from his lodging in the town, which was nothing inferior to any other nobleman's easement, and placed him in her house in the chamber directly under her own.

Darnley did not come in haste. He was not in Stirling, but hunting in the west, when Mary fell ill, and he did not arrive at Jedburgh until 28 October, more than ten days after Mary had taken ill. Admittedly, it may have been difficult to trace him with the news. Bothwell, of course, had just been seriously injured in the course of his duties as lieutenant of the Borders, and surely deserved a lodging superior to 'any other nobleman's easement'.

In the month of November 1566 she came to Craigmillar. The King, her husband, not ceasing his affectionate love and favour towards her, came thither, offering himself as became the husband to the wife. But when he had there continued a certain space, he neither found her passion and choler mitigated nor by any his good behaviour could procure her loving countenance and permission to pass to bed with her, but, partly persuaded and partly threatened to return to Stirling, as the place appointed for his exile and purgatory, he was willed as before no ways to have intelligence or resort to the foreign ambassadors until the time of the baptism, under pretext and colour that his garments were not prepared.

Darnley did visit Mary at Craigmillar.

When in December the appointed time of the baptism approached, the Queen passed to Stirling again, which solemnity she prepared and gave to Bothwell out of her own coffers and bought with her own money divers rich habiliments, at the device and fashioning whereof herself was master of work, and took no less care to have the same adorned above the state of the remaining noblemen than if she had been his bound servant. And on the other part not only was the King, her lawful husband, left desolate without any kind of preparation devised or made for him to the advancement of his honour in the time of such a triumph, but he was purposely restrained from access to the foreign ambassadors and they willed to forbear society with him, being all day within the castle of Stirling, as also the noblemen of Scotland and some officers that by her own appointment were directed or before to attend on his service at the time of the said baptism were inhibited either to accompany him or show him good usage or courtesy.

All the evidence is that it was of his own volition that Darnley took no part in the baptismal festivities. One reason may have been his fear, not without cause, that the English envoys would not recognise him as King. Another possible reason for this, as for Mary's avoidance of his company in the past weeks, may be that his features showed too clearly the marks of the syphilis from which he almost certainly suffered.

This her unnatural dealing in the sight and audience of foreign princes' ambassadors so far dejected him in courage that desperately he departed out of Stirling to Glasgow, where his father then made residence. But before his departure, to augment his grief in evident declaration of her indurate disdain, she caused her master of the household and others her officers to take from him all the plate and silver vessels that were appointed for him the time of their marriage and which had been occupied for his use and service continually thereafter, and in place thereof caused deliver pewter plates and vessels, and caused the servants appointed by her order to await on him to leave his service and company.

During the which whole time, but especially after the delivery of her birth, she so proceeded and continued in her disdain that she could not be content any nobleman or gentleman or familiar servant of her house should do honour to the King, her husband, use familiarity or company with him or convoy him on the high road, and if any did, incontinent she conceived such suspicion of them that they tasted of her evil will and bitter indignation. And, because her chief study and travail was to retain him from her company and out of her presence, she committed him as it were to ward, first during her keeping bed in Dalkeith after her birth and thereafter in Stirling continually until the baptism, from which places when sometimes he repaired towards her, as particularly is before expressed, she discharged her officers to furnish him any kind of expenses, concluding he should have nothing but in the room where she willed him to abide and remain. Which dejection and solitary state, joined with his poverty and necessity of needful things, may be counted not only exile and hostile banishment from the court but also a strait and miserable ward to a personage of his birth, age and calling. In all this time Bothwell governed both the court and public affairs, so that without his influence no nobleman or other subject had place of free speech with the Queen, or credit, or expected the least suit they could make.

There is some confirmation of the statement that by the end of 1566 insufficient money was allowed to Darnley for his ordinary expenses and the maintenance of his servants.

THE SECOND PART,
CONCERNING THE SAID QUEEN'S
INORDINATE AFFECTION BORNE TO JAMES,
SOMETIME EARL BOTHWELL, IN THE LIFETIME OF
THE KING, HER HUSBAND, BOTH BEFORE
AND AFTER HIS MURDER.

As her disdain began against the King, her lawful husband, whom by God's ordinance she ought to have preferred in honour and government before all others, she promoted Bothwell to the office of lieutenant general over all the Borders and made him general of her men of war, causing their captains of footmen to give their oath to him and make their whole dependence upon him.

Bothwell's father, Earl Patrick, had been appointed lieutenant of the Borders by Mary of Guise, and Earl James was lieutenant under her government in October 1558. On Mary's return the lieutenancy went to the Lord James. However, it is true that Bothwell was appointed lieutenant of all three marches by Mary by 21 September 1565.

Whereas no provision was devised for the support and sustentation of the King, her husband's, honourable estate (a sober pension out of the bishopric of Ross excepted), she gratified Bothwell with the rents of the abbeys of Melrose, Haddington and North Berwick, with promise of the abbey of Scone how soon the same shall fall vacant and become in her hands by consent of the demissioner or decease of the possessor thereof, his kinsman.

No reference is made here to the fact that Darnley's earldom of Ross, conferred in 1565, was no empty title, but included lands and their revenues. Darnley received the whole properties of the bishopric of Ross on 21 May 1565, but John Lesley was installed in the temporality of the bishopric on 20 April 1566, presumably with reservation of a pension to Darnley. Bothwell's interest in Melrose went much further back than the Book of Articles suggests, for he received a gift of it in March 1561, and in September of that year he tried to wrest it from the Earl of Arran, who was evidently holding it without a legal title, but in October he transferred his claim to Lord Robert Stewart. Michael Balfour became commendator of Melrose, but he had undertaken to grant a charter of the lands of the abbey to Bothwell. North Berwick was granted to Bothwell on 30 June 1566. Haddington had for a generation and more been almost an appanage of the house of Hepburn. When Earl James was temporarily out of favour, Lethington obtained it, but Bothwell subsequently reasserted his family's rights and cause another Hepburn prioress to be instituted. The commendator of Scone was Patrick Hepburn, Bothwell's great-uncle, and it would have been quite in acordance with current practice to promise the succession to another Hepburn.

In March 1565 she gave and disponed heritably to Bothwell the lands and lordship of Dunbar, with the heritable keeping thereof, which then was delivered into his hands with the whole powder and a great part of the munition of the realm of Scotland, the same lands and lordship being of the proper patrimony annexed to the crown and specially assigned to the sustentation of her house.

The gift of Dunbar to Bothwell is recorded on 24 March 1565–6.

In September 1566, she being at Master John Balfour's house in the Canongate and the Exchequer House within Edinburgh, Bothwell had continual access to her both night and day, when as the King, her husband, was hostilely removed and secluded from her society, not suffered to remain with her an hour. Her behaviour in the said Exchequer House showed forth how at that time she abused her body with him, he resorting through Master David Chalmer's lodging, where she lay, convoyed to her by means of the Lady Reres, which herself has confessed to diverse [times], and especially, he breaking the appointed tryst at one time, and she impatient of his tarry and delay sent the said Lady Reres to his chamber for him, which lady passing over the dyke at the nearest took him out of the bed from his wife and brought him to the Queen.

In the first place, Mary had official business at the Exchequer House, 'to understand her revenues and arrange for the maintenance of the prince'. It appears to be true that Bothwell was in Edinburgh at the time, but there is no contemporary allegation of any impropriety, and if there was the parties must have been highly discreet, for at the end of the month of September the privy council told Darnley that he should be thankful that he had such a virtuous wife. In the more expansive version of the alleged incidents which Buchanan gives in his Detectio, *he piles improbability upon improbability, characterising Lady Reres as 'a most dissolute woman, who had been one of Bothwell's whores and . . . in her old age had turned from the profession of harlotry to that of procuress' and describing her as 'a woman of ample weight in both years and body' – an unlikely candidate for climbing over a wall or, as the* Detectio *has it, being let down by a sash into the next garden. Buchanan professes to rely for his evidence on the confession of Bothwell's follower Dalgleish, but the latter's extant confession makes no mention of this episode.*

In October following, the year of God 1566, being in Borthwick, as she was intended to pass to Jedburgh, she heard of Bothwell's hurting to the death in Liddesdale, whereat she was so astonished that, uttering her inordinate affection, she departed in haste, first to Melrose, then to Jedburgh, never taking kindly rest until she came to the Hermitage in Liddesdale, and saw him, without respect of the intemperance of the weather and tempestuous air, the length and difficulty of the way or the danger of her person among the hands of notorious thieves and traitors. Through which excess, returning to Jedburgh, she fell in a heavy and grievous sickness, wherein to all man's appearance she was dead, and advertisement thereof passed by post into France.

Mary probably received the news of Bothwell's injuries not at Borthwick but at Jedburgh, to which town she had travelled by Borthwick and Melrose and where she arrived on 9 or 10 October. At any rate, it was from Jedburgh that she rode to Hermitage Castle, but not until 15 or possibly 16 October, more than a week after Bothwell had been wounded. It is true that the ride from Jedburgh to Hermitage and back in a day – over sixty miles – brought on the most serious of Mary's many illnesses. But, so far from being in the company only of those whom her enemies re-

garded as 'thieves and traitors', the Earl of Moray was with her on her visit to Hermitage.

What inordinate care she took to prepare all things for his transporting from the Hermitage to Jedburgh and for his easement there, but chiefly how before he was convalesced of his hurts she caused him be transported out of the lodging appointed for him and be placed within her house directly under her own chamber, where she spared not to visit him even before her convalescing, and how familiarly they had company together at that time in very suspicious manner they that were present perceived, and the world in those same days began to speak of it, comparing Bothwell's entertainment with that which the King, her husband, received at her hands when he came from Stirling to visit her.

The intelligible and reputable reasons for Mary's solicitude for Bothwell have already been mentioned on pp. 116–17. The two convalescents – Mary from an illness which had brought her to the point of death and Bothwell from wounds which had at first been thought fatal – seem improbable candidates for love-making at this point.

From Jedburgh as she journeyed through the Merse the night she lay in Coldingham the Lady Reres was intercepted coming through the watch who were in company with her, and where she intended to pass they knew well that met with her and the purpose was not altogether unknown to such as at that time attended in the Queen's company.

At the baptism of the King, now our sovereign lord, and before the same, it was marvellous to behold the Queen's care and solicitude taken for preparation of apparel and rich garments to Bothwell, of her own stuff, by her own device and commanding of the craftsmen, when as no kind of thing was appointed for the King in apparel, furniture or otherwise, but he hostilely sequestrated from all society of the foreign ambassadors being within Stirling Castle at once.

Other nobles besides Bothwell received gifts at this time. Darnley's position has already been discussed on p. 117.

The time of the said baptism she caused begin to make a passage between her chamber in the new work or palace within the castle of Stirling and the great hall thereof, thinking to have had access at all times by that means to Bothwell, whom purposely she caused to be lodged at the north end of the said great hall, as evidently appeared to all that were present for the time, and as the unperfected work this day testifies, which was left off by reason it could not be ended and serve to their commodity, for that they departed out of Stirling before it could be perfect.

As no accounts of the master of works or other records of royal building operations are extant at this point, it is impossible to confirm this statement.

The same time, because sundry gentlemen of the Lennox and others, the King's friends, resorted to Stirling during the solemnity of the baptism, Bothwell took such fear that he caused twelve or fourteen servants to lie round about his bed in arms, and she, moved by the grudge of her guilty conscience, conceiving the like fear and suspicion for the said earl, commanded Gilbert Balfour, his master household for the time, to bring within the castle fifty harquebusses for Bothwell's guard, who coming to the castle gate without knowledge of the Earl of Mar, captain thereof, he refused to give them entry.

Bothwell's measures seem not unreasonable precautions against the Lennox faction. Mar's action, since the keeping of the castle was his responsibility, is quite intelligible.

When she understood that the Earl of Moray intended to convoy the Earl of Bedford, ambassador for the Queen's Majesty of England, through Fife to his house at St Andrews, she willed the said Earl of Moray to desire Bothwell to accompany them to St Andrews, that it might appear they were good friends; which according to her desire my said Earl of Moray, now Regent, did, and Bothwell condescended,* but neither he nor the Queen minding such thing they departed together towards Drymen, the Lord Drummond's house, abiding there five or six days, and from that came to Tullibardine. In what order they were chambered during their remaining in these two houses many found fault with it that dared not reprove it. How lascivious also their behaviour was it was very strange to behold, notwithstanding of the news of the King's grievous infirmity, who was departed to Glasgow and there fallen into deadly sickness.

Mary was at Drymen on 28 December and at Tullibardine on 31 December, but there seems to be no support for the allegations of impropriety at those places.

Returning to Stirling, and still continuing in her inordinate affection to Bothwell, she thought she could not sufficiently persuade him of her favour unless she delivered her son also into his hands as a pledge thereof. And for that purpose she began to find fault with the prince's lodging as lacking good air, and in the extremity of the cold winter caused him to be transported out of the castle of

* I.e., agreed.

Stirling to the palace of Holyroodhouse where he was under the guard of Bothwell and the soldiers who were ever at his commandment, and especially by the time that the Queen rode towards Glasgow to convoy the King to Edinburgh.

Mary brought the prince with her to Edinburgh on 14 January. Her action is capable of an innocent explanation, in view of the rumours which were afoot that Darnley intended to crown the prince and govern in his name or even a suspicion that Darnley might do away with the prince. It was not unreasonable to believe that the child would be safer with Bothwell.

Finally this her inordinate affection to Bothwell, beginning as she entered into disdain with the King, her husband, continued not only to his murder, but the said Bothwell's place, credit and authority were in such estimation with her that only he had the management of all the public affairs and without his knowledge nothing was expeded at the Queen's hands. And from September 1566 he became so familiar with her both night and day that at his pleasure he abused her body, to the consummation of the King, her husband's, murder, who in all that time was never permitted to remain patiently the space of forty-eight hours together in her company, but, when he endeavoured to remain and attend upon her according to the husband's duty, by excuses, persuasions or sharp menacings he was compelled to retire to such places as she appointed, Bothwell in the mean time remaining in company with her and using all things at his pleasure.

Of the which disdain and extreme hatred conceived against her husband, and inordinate affection borne to Bothwell, with whom she abused her body in her said husband's lifetime in manner above expressed, necessarily follows the compassing and deliberation taken of his death and destruction and consequently the execution of his murder.

This is a mere summing up of the section, and requires no comment.

THE THIRD PART,
CONTAINING THE CONSPIRACY
DEVISED AND EXECUTION OF THE SAID KING'S
HORRIBLE MURDER BY THE QUEEN,
HIS WIFE, AND BOTHWELL.

After long disdain continued against the King, her husband, and inordinate affection borne to Bothwell, increased her indurate and deadly hatred against the King in such sort that she, impatient longer to be abstracted from abusing her body in public manner with Bothwell, at the occasion of a letter written to her by the King, which she received being at Kelso in her progress as she returned from Jedburgh about the beginning of November 1566, she burst out in direct words to my lord, now Regent, the Earl of Huntly and the Secretary, sorely weeping and tormenting herself miserably as if she would have fallen into her sickness, and said that unless she were quit of the King by one means or other she could never have a good day in her life, and rather, before she fell therein, to be the instrument of her own death.

There seems to be no specific evidence, independent of Buchanan's writings, for Mary's outburst as related here, but it finds some support in a report written by the French ambassador, at Edinburgh, on 2 December. Referring to Mary's condition when she had been at Craigmillar, a few days earlier, he said: 'She is in the hands of the physicians, and I do assure you is not at all well; and do believe the principal part of her disease to consist in a deep grief and sorrow . . . Still she repeats these words, "I could wish to be dead".'

In the same month, at her coming to Craigmillar, where she reposed a while before her passing to Stirling for the baptism, she renewed the same purpose which she spoke of before at Kelso, in the audience of the said Earl of Moray, now Regent, the Earls of Huntly, Argyll and the Secretary, proposing that the best way to be quit of the King, her husband, was by divorce, which might easily be brought to pass through the consanguinity standing between them, the dispensation being abstracted, which she caused be sought and brought before purposely to that end. But seeing it answered how that could not be goodly done without hazard that the prince, her son, should be declared bastard, since neither the King, her husband, nor she contracted that marriage as ignorant of the degrees of consanguinity wherein they stood, she utterly left that conceit and opinion of divorce and ever from that day forth imagined and devised how to cut him away by death.

This is a version of the 'Craigmillar Conference', discussed in chapter 2 (pp. 30–31), but its conclusion does not accord with the other evidence for that conference – which, admittedly, was framed by Mary or her supporters.

And first, in the beginning of December 1566, at her coming to Stirling for the baptism, she caused the King, her husband, remove out of William Bell's lodging to the castle, and there placed him in an obscure and narrow room at no better estate than a prisoner, during all the time that the ambassadors remained there, to whom he had never access, but remained covertly until his departing to Glasgow, being all the time served of his meat out of the Queen's kitchen by her officers and servants. What he received there God knows, but immediately after his departing out of Stirling, before he had ridden half a mile, he fell into so grievous and so uncouth sickness as he was despaired of his life, but yet rode forward to Glagsow and lay there all the time thereafter, until she drew him to Edinburgh. That it was poison that grieved him appeared by the breaking out of his body and many other circumstances which also James Abernethy, surgeon, at the sight of him plainly judged and spoke. In this also appeared her cruelty that she refused to send her mediciner or apothecary to visit him.

The possible reasons for Darnley's seclusion at Stirling have already been discussed (p. 117 above). It has been observed that to 'ride forward' when his life was despaired of was something of an achievement. Reports that Darnley had been poisoned were widespread, but this was almost a convention when illustrious persons fell ill in those days. Contrary to the allegation here, the Earl of Bedford reported that Mary sent her own physician to Darnley.

But this his marvellous sickness (in all men's judgements seeming rather artificial than natural) was yet overcome by youth and nature, and she, hearing of his convalescing, took purpose with Bothwell in Edinburgh to pass to Glasgow and bring the King to Edinburgh. And she, being at Glasgow travailing to bring the King with her, she wrote to Bothwell to see if he might find out a more secret [way] by medicine to cut him off than that way which between them they had conspired and devised of his destruction before her coming from Edinburgh.

The allegation that Mary suggested 'a more secret way to cut him off' is one of the points in which the Book of Articles agrees with the Casket Letters (p. 54 above).

For it appears well they had devised the fatal house for him before she rode to Glasgow, with whom passed Bothwell and the Earl of Huntly until she came to Callendar, and there remaining with her a night they returned to Edinburgh and she rode forward to Glasgow. But Bothwell at his coming to Edinburgh lodged in the town, where by custom he used to lie at the abbey, and rising in the morning timeous he passed directly to the Kirk o' Field, to visit and consider the house prepared for the King, where he was found by divers who for sundry affairs sought him that morning. And he was right sore offended that any should have found him there. And from Glasgow by her letters and otherwise she held him continually in remembrance of the said house.

The allegation that 'the fatal house' had been selected for Darnley before Mary left for Glasgow is hard to reconcile with other evidence, and indeed inconsistent with the Casket Letters, which are explicit that Craigmillar was the proposed destination. For a discussion of the responsibility for the choice of Kirk o' Field, see p. 35 above.

Being in Glasgow, suddenly she altered her forward countenance and disdain, long continued against her husband into dissembled reconciliation and hearty entertainment. And howbeit he was not thoroughly convalesced and nothwithstanding that he feared his life (as she herself writes) and was minded to pass out of Scotland, yet upon her promise and treasonable dealing she enticed and persuaded him to come to Edinburgh with her, where his death and destruction were concluded and after executed between her and Bothwell.

The sudden change in Mary's attitude to Darnley was clearly so startling as to demand some explanation, but the suggestions made here seem less convincing than those put forward in chapter 2 (p. 34 above).

And in declaration that it was only her craft and subtle persuasion that drew him out of Glasgow, as they were riding forth the way by Kilsyth she passed before, desiring him to follow after her in the litter. But he, even then suspecting his life, said he would return to Glasgow if she tarried not with him, and she, not willing to spoil the purpose that was so far brought to pass, [not] only returned to him but alighted and gave him meat out of her own hands.

There appears to be no independent confirmation of this.

Yet she had no will to pass into Edinburgh until she knew assuredly that the house where the King's lodging and all other things needful for the murder were prepared, wherefore she remained at Linlithgow until Hob Ormiston, one of the murderers, who is condemned therefor, came to her, declaring that Bothwell was returned to Edinburgh and had prepared all things.

This is irreconcilable with the confessions of Ormiston and other followers of Bothwell, who testified not to careful preparations in advance but to hasty and muddled operations on the eve of the murder (p. 47 above).

At her coming to Edinburgh she convoyed the King to the appointed lodging, but he of accident riding a little before her alighted in the kirkyard of the Kirk o' Field and passed directly to the Duke of Châtelherault's lodging because it was the most goodly house he saw nearest the church, thinking it therefore to be prepared for him. But the Archbishop of St Andrews purposely lodged in it at that time only to debar the King from it, and the Queen finding him standing at the gate of the Duke's house desired him and caused him come to the other unworthy house prepared for his destruction, which was unmeet in all respects for any honest man to lodge in, situated in a solitary place at the outmost part of the town, ruinous, waste and not inhabited by any of a long time before, and subject on all sides to evident peril, having four several entrances, at every one of which his evil-willers might easily have access, one of them through the town wall, another eastward towards the Blackfriars' yard, the third through the chaplains' chamber and the fourth the front entrance.

The question whether Darnley expected to be lodged in the Duke's house was discussed in chapter 2 (p. 42 above). That the Old Provost's Lodging, where he actually took up residence, was 'unmeet in all respects for any honest man to lodge in' and was 'ruinous and waste' is hard to accept, in view of the fact that the room below Darnley's was considered fit for the Queen herself. It is also difficult to reconcile the description of the premises with the statement in the next paragraph that they were amply supplied with keys.

To the effect that the horrible murder thus conspired might the more easily be done, there were double keys made of the whole doors of the said house and delivered into the hands of John of Bolton, servant to Bothwell, who was one of the chief executors of the murder with his hands. But the keys of the door between the King's chamber and the house under it where the Queen lay and where the powder was put in were delivered to Archibald Beaton and Paris, Frenchman, the Queen's own chamber-servants.

The information about the duplicate keys is in accordance with the deposition of Bothwell's follower, Bolton, who said that he had fourteen 'false keys' for opening all the doors of the King's lodging. Buchanan's History, however, by stating that Darnley's servants 'could not get possession of the keys to the doors from those who had prepared the lodging' may seem to contradict the statement that duplicates were made. The deposition of Darnley's servant, Nelson, was that the keys of the lodging were delivered to him by Robert Balfour, owner of the property, except the key of the door which passed through the cellar and the town wall, which could not be found. These keys were kept by Nelson and used by him and other servants of the King until the Queen came to the lodging. Then the key of her room and the key of the passage to the garden were delivered to Archibald Beaton, usher of the

*Queen's chamber. The whole business of the keys is extremely
confusing.*

But to abuse the world by appearance of that new reconciliation
between her and her husband to the end the having of certain
keys of the lodging should not be found suspicious in her servants'
hands, she lay in the house under the King, where also thereafter
the powder was placed, being an unmeet place for a prince to
lodge in, two nights, viz. the Wednesday and Friday before his
murder, which was then concluded to have been executed on the
Friday at night, but yet stayed partly because the preparations
were not all ready and partly in respect of another method, which
she practised upon Saturday at afternoon, between the King and
my Lord of Holyroodhouse, thinking it more seemly to have her
husband cut off by such an accident proceeding in contention than
by the powder and raising of the house.

*The question of the true location of the powder was discussed
in chapter 2 (p. 36). The postponing of the murder, though from
the Saturday, not the Friday, to the Sunday night, and with a
different explanation, is mentioned in the deposition of Hay of
Tallo.*

For on Saturday she spoke to the King concerning some communication that had been between him and the said Lord Robert,
and the same denied by him she brought them together in the
King's chamber the same day at afternoon, and there confronting
them never left to provoke the one against the other until in her
own presence from words she caused them offer strokes and in her
it stood not but they had made end of the matter even there,
nothing caring who should be victor but thinking, the one being
slain, the other should shortly follow, judging the same the most
commodious means to colour the murder enterprised, which in her
letters to Bothwell she terms 'our affairs'.

*The quarrel between Darnley and Lord Robert is mentioned
also in the* Detectio, *the 'Indictment' prepared by Lennox, and
Buchanan's History, but only in the last is it stated that Lord
Robert told Darnley of Mary's plan for the murder and that
Darnley passed this on to the Queen, whereupon Lord Robert
denied it and Moray was called in 'in the hope that he also would
perish on the same occasion'. A letter purporting to show that
Mary fostered the quarrel was produced at York, but seems to
have been withheld at Westminster.*

Upon the Sunday at night she and Bothwell supped in Mr John
Balfour's house in the Canongate, where the Bishop of the Isles
made banquet, from which Bothwell passed directly to the laird of

Ormiston's chamber above the bow* in Edinburgh, and there with the said laird, Hob Ormiston, his father's brother, John Hepburn of Bolton and John Hay, younger, of Tallo, devised and concluded upon the convoying of the powder towards the King's house. The Queen passed up the way to that same house and gave the King all manner of entertainment to colour the act whereof the execution followed so near, for she said she would lie there all night; howbeit in the meantime Paris, her familiar servant in her chamber, was in the lower house where she lay the nights preceding, and opened the door thereof, taking in the powder and the murderers thereas, for he kept the key that opened to that entrance of the garden. And because there was a bed and some tapestry of value in that lodging, set up for the King before his coming thereto, she caused remove the same by the keepers of her wardrobe to Holyroodhouse on the Friday preceding the murder, and another worse was set up in the place thereof, which she thought good enough to be expended in such use, seeing it was destined for the same.

The banquet given by the Bishop of the Isles is authenticated in the account of Bothwell's movements recounted in the depositions of his followers, with which the above paragraph is substantially in accordance. It seems that a bed of 'black figured velvet' had been among the spoils Mary collected from the Earl of Huntly's residence at Strathbogie in the Corrichie campaign in 1562, and it was 'a new bed of black figured velvet' which was provided for Darnley at Kirk o' Field and removed by Mary before the murder, to be replaced by an old portable purple bed. Lennox's 'Narrative' explained that Mary said to Darnley that they would share the new bed when he joined her at Holyrood. One deposition says that the reason for the removal was to prevent the good new bed being spoiled by the splashing when Darnley had his bath. The best comment on this subject is that by Eric Linklater in his Mary, Queen of Scots: 'There is a domestic detail, small enough, but of some interest in connexion with this assumption that Mary's behaviour was simply dictated by womanly zeal for nursing: in Darnley's room there was a new black bed, and this Mary had removed, lest the splashing of his bath should spoil it, and substituted for it an old purple couch. Her enemies have assumed that this indicates her foreknowledge of his murder and her desire to save the new bed from destruction by the explosion. But surely to believe that requires the belief that Mary was not only a murderess but a mean and grasping murderess? That she would count the

---

* Presumably Netherbow, the arched gateway separating Edinburgh from the Canongate.

cost of killing, and tell Bothwell in what shop gunpowder was selling at bargain prices? There is nothing in her history to substantiate such a view. She was not parsimonious. The woman who pawned her jewels to pay her soldiers would not grudge a bedstead when it came to murdering her husband. But if Mary were behaving merely as a good wife would behave, the substitution of the beds is perfectly comprehensible. She was simply being sensible in a 'sound domestic way.'

The powder being laid in the lower house, whereat Bothwell in his own person was present, he came therefrom to the King's chamber. And after he had played at the dice a while with the other lords who attended there on the Queen, Paris came up out of her chamber and gave a sign that all was prepared, which so soon as she perceived (being kissing and familiarly entertaining the King, at which time she put a ring on his finger) she said, 'I have failed Bastian, that this night of his marriage promised him the masque'; and so incontinent cried for horses and departed towards Holyroodhouse, Bothwell being in her company.

That Mary gave Darnley a ring on leaving him is well attested. Mary's sudden recollection of her undertaking to Bastian has never seemed a very likely explanation of her departure from Kirk o' Field. Some of her courtiers and servitors must have known her intended movements. Besides, one very circumstantial report says that she was masked when she was with Darnley, and this suggests that she had only temporarily left the festivities and did not suddenly remember Bastian's wedding. Mary certainly told Archbishop Beaton that it was a mere chance that she had escaped the explosion, but does this necessarily confirm her sudden recollection of her engagement?

All the way until her coming to the palace, and after her alighting in her own chamber, she held purpose with Bothwell only until after 12 hours in the night, for the laird of Traquair, captain of the guard, being the last man that tarried in the chamber that night, left them together and passed to his bed. After which Bothwell departed as it had been to his bed in the Lord Ruthven's house, which had passage both within and without the palace, and incontinent changed his hose and doublet and passed without delay to the execution of the murder, which being done he returned directly to his said chamber at the palace, passing and repassing by her watch.

There is no independent confirmation of the first part of this paragraph. The second part is in accordance with the depositions of Bothwell's followers.

The murder thus continued in a strange and uncouth manner, notwithstanding the horrible crack of the powder in the overthrow and raising of the house, which astonished and awakened the most part of the inhabitants of the town, yet it neither alarmed nor moved the Queen no more than such a thing had never been.

Thereafter Bothwell being raised out of his bed by Mr George Halket, his man, coming out [. . .]* before his master slept, the said Bothwell and certain other lords and ladies lying in the palace passed to the Queen's chamber and declared the King was dead, yet she was little altered or abased at that strange news, but desired them to pass to the town and see the manner, and thereafter slept soundly, doors and windows all closed, not asking further news until 12 hours at noon.

That the Queen was not disturbed by the explosion is not confirmed, and there seems to be no evidence as to who gave her the news. It will be noted that this account says nothing specifically of the manner of Darnley's death, but naturally implies that he perished in the explosion which Bothwell and Mary had engineered.

The same Monday, which was the 12 February 1566, at afternoon, the matter being wondered at and great execration in the mouths of the multitude against the authors of that mischievous act, for the sake of appearance a council was convened in the Earl of Argyll's chamber to make some show of enquiry, where Thomas Nelson and some others that lay in the King's house were enquired among other things who prepared and ordained that house for the King, others asked who had the keys. To whom the said Nelson answered that there were certain keys, namely that they were in the hands of the Queen's servants, Archibald Beaton and Paris, which neither he nor any other servant of the King ever received; which the laird of Tullibardine, comptroller, hearing, said 'There is a ground'. But Bothwell and others of the council perceiving the peril, never dipped further in the trial and enquiry, but grudged at the Earl of Atholl and the comptroller in such sort that it behoved them for fear of their lives to leave the court, whereunto

* One or two words missing.

they never returned during the said Earl Bothwell's bearing of rule.

Monday was actually the 10th. The reference to an immediate enquiry before Argyll, who was Justice General and nominally responsible for criminal justice, finds some support in the existence of depositions dated 11 February. Atholl (who was very much a Lennox man) and Tullibardine had left the court by 26 February and were ordered to return.

Upon the morning after the murder, which was Tuesday the 11th day, Margaret Carwood, the Queen's familiar and secret servant (whose great credit in all things is not unknown to our adversaries), was married within the Queen's palace and the banquet made on the Queen's charges, which declared that the mourning for the King soon decayed, and there was on the days following more travail prepared for the investigation of certain money stolen from the said Margaret than for the King's murder recently committed.

A cogent reason for not deferring the wedding was that 11 February was Shrove Tuesday, and the disapproval of marriage in Lent survived the reformation. It is true that Mary did pay for the festivities, but the payment would certainly have been arranged before Darnley's death.

The King's person was left lying in the yard where it was apprehended the space of three hours, no man once pressing to carry the same away, until the rascal people transported him to a vile house near that room where he was lodged before, where he remained 48 hours as a gazing stock, without any care taken of him saving certain [...]* purposely set to keep the entry that his corpse should not be seen by the multitude, fearing that they, moved by the sight, should have been induced suddenly to make uproar.

There was purpose held in council of his honourable burial, and conclusion taken that his corpse should be taken and brought to the chapel within the palace of Holyroodhouse and there remain until preparation might be made for his burial and honourable entertainment, which should not have been accomplished until the end of forty days. Notwithstanding, in manifest declaration of her continued hatred against his dead body, she caused the same to be brought from the Kirk o' Field to the said chapel of Holyroodhouse by certain soldiers, pioneers and other vile persons, upon an old block of form or tree. And after that the corpse had lain certain days in the chapel, where also she beheld it, the same corpse with-

* One or two words missing.

out any decent order was cast into the earth in the night, without any ceremony or company of honest men.

No mention is made here of the fact that Darnley's body was duly embalmed, as usual with royal personages, by 12 February. The Queen paid for mourning clothes on 15 February. The account of the burial given here is on the whole confirmed by contemporary and near-contemporary authorities: 'quietly in the night, without any kind of solemnity or mourning'; 'beside King James the Fifth, in his sepulture, quietly'. It is true that the reformers were opposed to funeral solemnities, and it was therefore inconsistent of them to criticise the lack of ceremonial. Bishop Lesley indeed said that the 'quietness' of the burial was to meet objections from the Protestant lords. The 'quietness' may, however, have arisen from genuine doubt as to what kind of obsequies could properly be held, in view of the equivocal religious attitude of the deceased. In the end there was a mass and a dirge on 23 March, the first Sunday after the expiry of the forty days of mourning.

This unworthy usage of the King's body and the oversight and neglecting of trial in inquisition for his murder moved the common people to affix placards secretly in all public places naming and declaring the murderers, chiefly Bothwell, who was always the better favoured and had place to call and trouble all painters and others suspected for working or affixing of the said placards. So that all the investigation that duly ought to have been taken for the King's murder was turned and used against the up-putters of the said placards, which notwithstanding from time to time continued. Yet, lest it should appear that nothing at all was done for the murder, there was a proclamation set forth promising a thousand pounds to any that would reveal the murderers, which was not long unanswered, for by a new placard it was offered that the money being consigned in an impartial hand the murderers should be revealed and the avower should utter his name, yet nothing followed. But in the parliament she set forth an act against the affixers of the said placards, making the doing thereof a crime of *lèse majesté*. And at the pronunciation of the act in the parliament house, said that if she were the woman whom the placards named she was not only unworthy to reign over so ancient a people, but was also unworthy to live on the face of the earth.

The setting up of the placards is amply demonstrated. The proclamation of the reward for information about the murderers was issued on 12 February. An act against placards was passed by parliament in April.

Howbeit the Earl of [Lennox, the] King's father, many times wrote to her not only requiring the murder to be tried but also naming Bothwell in special and certain others of the murderers, and craving that they might be put in ward until the end of the trial, yet she utterly neglected, shifted and delayed the same, and wilfully retained the named and known murderer of her husband in her company in chiefest honour and familiarity, rewarding his servants and accomplices at all occasions.

Lennox did write to Mary as here alleged. Bothwell did receive gifts on 1 March and again at the end of the month. On the other hand, he was only one of many nobles (including Moray) in whose favour acts were passed in the April parliament.

But seeing the incessant crying of my lord Earl of Lennox for justice, so directly touching the Earl Bothwell, her chief minion, with whom she had now obliged herself to marry, yea as well appears before the murder of her husband, unto the which marriage without some form of purgation of Bothwell thinking it [not] decent for her to proceed, some of the council were therefore commanded to convene in Seton and consultation taken how and in what fashion he might be quit of the murder, whereupon letters were directed summoning the Earl of Lennox and all others having interest to pursue Bothwell on 40 days warning, against the order of the law in such cases observed, for the crime being treason as they that are called ought to be summoned on 40 days warning so if the suspected traitor suit his own purgation as Bothwell then did, the father, mother, wife, bairns, kin and friends of the murdered king ought to have been summoned to pursue on the like space of forty days, as the murderer might have claimed in case he had been directly pursued at their instance, and further because Lady Margaret, the king's mother, was out of the realm her premonition ought to have been on 60 days according to the laws of Scotland.

The Book of Articles itself has not previously suggested that Mary had promised to marry Bothwell before Darnley's death. The proclamation summoning Lennox and others to pursue Bothwell for the murder was dated 28 March, and the trial was fixed for 12 April, which certainly did not give forty days warning.

Yet impatient of the delay of that unlawful marriage, whereunto she intended with the murderer of her husband, after the summons had been directed and before the day that the murderer underlay the law, he being possessed of a lawful wife of his own, the Queen made the second contract of marriage with him, dated at Seton the 5 day of April and written by the Earl of Huntly 1567, subscribed by both their hands, as a reward and recompense of the murder which by her advice he had committed.

The contract bearing the date 5 April is referred to again later in the Book of Articles (p. 137 below). It has been suggested that it was genuine but that Mary refused to sign it, but its character is so peculiar, at least in the copy of it which survives, that its authenticity may be questioned.

Upon the 12 day of April 1567, appointed to try for the fashion the murderer by the law, divers nobleman and others, knowing what was intended and suiting to escape the strait, earnestly travailed that they should not be on the assize or inquest, notwithstanding they were compelled by the Queen extraordinary to be present at the action and to be of the number of the same inquest.

This looks like a retrospective justification of those who had taken part. However, on 20 December 1567 the Earl of Caithness, who had been foreman of the jury, protested on behalf of himself and his fellow jurors that they had made a protestation at the time that the evidence had not been adequate to justify Bothwell's condemnation.

Where of duty she ought to have taken special care and utter diligence for the pursuit of her husband's murder, by the contrary her soldiers were appointed to attend on Bothwell's person as a guard for his defence when he passed and returned to and from the tolbooth,* her advocates also were expressly forbidden to prosecute him, and to the end the matter should have passed forward without stop or contradiction they accused him of a murder committed on the ninth day, the King's murder indeed being committed on the tenth day. The indictment was also presented against him unsworn. And, notwithstanding the earnest solicitation of my lord Earl of Lennox, but also of the Queen's Majesty of England's request sent for deferring of that day, in consideration of that inordinate and partial proceeding intended, until a time more opportune, all was utterly refused, because nothing was regarded but once to have [him] acquitted by one means or other, that the marriage might follow.

Bothwell's indictment does give the date of the murder as 9 February. Elizabeth's messenger arrived early on the day of the trial, and did not receive an audience of Mary on his arrival. It was not unreasonable to ignore the intervention of a foreign power.

Before this time was a counterfeited mourning, which albeit it lasted scarce eight days of forty that according to the custom of princes are due, yet the ceremony was so ill observed even in the

---

* The town-house o court-house, where trials were held.

eight and ten days after the murder that Harry Killigrew, the Queen's Majesty of England's servant, deprehended the order of the house all perturbed as he came to the Queen's presence (then for the manner's sake keeping the bed), howbeit in his access he was not sudden nor indiscreet. So difficult it is to feign mourning out of a joyous heart.

Killigrew did not have his first audience of Mary until 8 March, nearly a month after the murder.

A few days after the murder remaining at Holyroodhouse, she passed to Seton, exercising herself one day right openly at the fields with the pell mell and golf, and on the night plainly abusing her body with Bothwell, who in that house was placed in a secret and obscure chamber directly under hers, having a secret passage between, by which he had access to her at his appetite, the said chamber being altogether unmeet for a nobleman of such state and credit as he bore at that time and there being many more sufficient houses beside the same occupied by mean men, if that chamber had not been used purposely to the effect abovespecified. And albeit Monsieur de Crocq, ambassador for the King of France, drew her out of Seton to Edinburgh, yet she thought the place of Seton so proper for their usage that short while tarrying at Edinburgh returned again to Seton.

The facts are that Mary went to Seton on 16 February, while Bothwell remained at Holyrood. She returned to Holyrood on 19 February, but was back at Seton, this time with Bothwell, before the 26th.

After the murder of the King, her husband, by advice of Bothwell and others, then her chief councillors, she thought not only that the earldom of Lennox was fallen into her hands by reason of ward through decease of the King, her husband, her son the prince now our sovereign lord being lawful and rightful heir thereof, but also she caused divers of the free tenants of the said earldom pay fines for the ward of their proper lands and disponed a part of the property thereof to the Lord Boyd.

It would appear that Darnley's father must have resigned the earldom to his son, reserving a life rent, and this would have provided some justification for claiming that the earldom was in ward in the minority of Prince James. However, there is little confirmation of the allegations made here except a gift of the ward of part of the lands of the earldom of Lennox to Lord Boyd.

Also she disponed her said deceased husband's horses, clothing, armour and whatsoever was his to Bothwell, his chief murderer, and others his known enemies, in manifest proof of her continued hatred against his dead body and of her favour borne to his murderers.

And to the end she might the more easily attain to the marriage of the murderer, which could not be until divorce was made and led between him and his lawful wife, the Earl of Huntly's sister, the Queen restored the said Earl of Huntly by parliament to his living, for which he persuaded his sister to subscribe a procuratory that the divorce might be pursued in her name.

It is true that Huntly did not obtain formal restitution of his earldom, which had been forfeited after his father's rebellion in 1562, until the parliament of April 1567. However, Huntly had long been restored to royal favour, and had indeed, as we have seen, been appointed chancellor in March 1566.

The Queen never ceased after the murder of her husband until she had the Earl of Mar displaced out of the castle of Edinburgh, who and his father had truly kept the same of a long continuance; and shortly placed the murderer therein and put the whole munitions of the realm in [. . .]*

The Earl of Mar did give up the keepership of Edinburgh Castle, but he was not succeeded by Bothwell. Actually Sir James Balfour of Pittendreich became keeper, and (despite his earlier association with Bothwell) denied Bothwell the use of the stronghold after his marriage to Mary.

The parliament of the Earl of Huntly's restitution being ended upon the 19 day of April 1567, the lords being called to supper by Bothwell at his house, then kept within the palace of Holyroodhouse, which was environed with his guard of men of war, after supper he proposed a bond to them to subscribe for advancing of him to the Queen's marriage, which they refusing to subscribe without her own advice and knowledge of her opinion she subscribed a letter at the first motion in token of her consent and goodwill, he then being possessed of a wife and the King, her husband, murdered little more than two months before. In which space she had passed two contracts to marry him, one without a date, the other of the fifth of April. And she desired the said letter of her consent to be kept secret.

The bond urging the marriage of Mary and Bothwell is not the least of the mysteries of the period. The supper was, according to most accounts, held not at Bothwell's quarters in the palace, but at Ainslie's Tavern. The signatories claimed afterwards that they had signed partly because the place was surrounded by 200 hagbutters and also because Bothwell produced Mary's warrant auth-

* One or two words missing, possibly 'his hands'.

orising them to sign. Moray's name appears in some lists of signatories, although he was out of the country at the time. A letter by Mary approving the bond was produced at York on 11 October 1568 but did not appear at Westminster, and it has not survived.

Next, for covering up of their ungodly filthy usage, continued a long time, they devised a counterfeited ravishing of her person, and for that purpose she rode to Stirling as it were to visit her son on Monday the 21 of April, and on the Wednesday returned at night to Linlithgow, he on the other part feigning him to ride in Liddesdale convened a company of armed men and according as had been before devised and as she wrote to him out of Linlithgow, he met her and ravished* her, conveying her in haste to Dunbar Castle, where he openly passed to bed with her, abusing her body at his pleasure. Which form of ravishing he practised also to his own advantage, thinking, it being a crime of *lèse majesté*, to take a remission therefor as he did, and under the same crime to comprehend the King's murder in case it might be tried thereafter.

No remission to Bothwell himself is recorded in the Register of the Privy Seal, *but on 10 May there were remissions to five men who had been associated with him in his seizure of the Queen, pardoning them for their part in the action and for all other crimes, without the exception of treason, which is commonly an exception in remissions. However, the suggestion that the object of the abduction of Mary was the obtaining of a comprehensive remission for Bothwell seems improbable, in view of the fact that he had already been judicially acquitted of Darnley's murder.*

Being thus led and detained as appeared captive in Dunbar, divers noblemen wrote to her, requiring to know the truth of her strange and irreverent handling, and offering to convene her forces and relieve her majesty, she plainly mocked at and showed no signs of discontent.

A little support for this allegation is to be found in a reference to an offer of help from loyal subjects in Aberdeen.

In the time of her remaining at Dunbar by the space of eight or nine days a divorce was led in two forms between Bothwell and his lawful wife, not without the Queen's earnest solicitation to the judges and others that might further the same, she notwithstanding professing herself captive; which divorcements well considered are null: that which is grounded on adultery upon his part for lack of proof and insufficiency of the witness; the other, for consanguinity standing between him and his wife, proceeded only because the

* I.e., abducted.

138

dispensation was abstracted, the poor man nominated judge being diverse times menaced of his life.

The dual actions for divorce were indeed carried through, and it is true that the dispensation for Bothwell's marriage to Lady Jean Gordon was suppressed (p. 53 above). But it is hard to believe that there was inadequate evidence of Bothwell's adultery with Bessie Crawford, his wife's sewing maid.

Sentence being pronounced in this unlawful divorce, she and Bothwell removed from Dunbar to the castle of Edinburgh, hastening by all means to accomplish the pretended marriage between them, and there made the third contract of marriage, gave him the earldom of Orkney and lordship of Shetland heritably, which of before she had disponed to her brother my lord Robert of Holyroodhouse. The reader also of the church of Edinburgh refusing to cry her banns she wrote commanding the same expressly to be done, abiding then in Edinburgh Castle.

Actually Mary entered Edinburgh on 6 May, the day before the sentence of divorce on grounds of consanguinity was pronounced. Bothwell was created Duke of Orkney on 12 May. There was a marriage contract on 14 May. The Book of Articles, with almost characteristic carelessness, attributes the reluctance to proclaim the banns to the 'reader' of the church of Edinburgh. A reader was a kind of unordained assistant, authorised to read the services; but the man who refused to proclaim the banns, until he received a direct order to do so, was John Craig, who was a minister. He had been appointed Knox's colleague, and was in charge of the church of St Giles at this time, Knox being in England.

And upon Monday the 12 of May, after her banns were cried, she came out to the castle to the tolbooth of Edinburgh and there, in presence of the Lords of Council and Session and divers noblemen, declared that albeit she was distressed for the present by her capture by Bothwell yet for his good behaviour towards her she stood content with him, declaring that she forgave him and his complices and declared herself at liberty, wherein his deep dissimulation may easily be espied.

Mary's declaration is authenticated, but Buchanan, in his History, places it before and not after the calling of the banns.

In all this time she never required the advice and opinion of her council and nobility towards her marriage, nor ever entered purpose thereof until the afternoon before it was accomplished, and then the same being proposed the lords that were present thought great evil of that form of proceeding and spoke in plain terms they could not approve the marriage unless the bond which was subscribed on the 19 of April were destroyed, for satisfaction of whom the Queen's consent to that bond was written upon the same paper and she subscribed it.

This is authenticated.

And upon Thursday the 15 day of May 1567 was the said pretended and unlawful marriage ended and accomplished in two fashions, which Monsieur du Crog, the French ambassador, so greatly disdained that, being lodged within a very short space to the palace of Holyroodhouse, he would not at the Queen's desire pass to the banquet.

If 'two fashions' is intended to mean that there was a Roman Catholic as well as a Protestant ceremony, it goes against the weight of the evidence in favour of a Protestant ceremony only.

So, apparently to our judgement, less presumptions than here are expressed should serve for the full probation of this matter. Considering that Queen Jane of Naples being of the like crime accused was adjudged culpable of the same, far fewer presumptions being laid to her charge, as it appears by the example of Louis, King of Hungary, answering the said queen, declares in these words: 'Inordinata vita precedens, retentio protestatis in regno, neglecta vindicta vir alter susceptus et excusatio subsequens: necis viri tui te probant fuisse participem et consortem.'

THE FIFTH AND LAST PART,
CONTAINING HOW BY OCCASION OF THE PUNISHMENT
OF THE SAID MURDER NEGLECTED,
THE NOBLEMEN AND OTHER GOOD SUBJECTS TOOK
ARMS, DETAINED AND SEQUESTRATED THE SAID
QUEEN'S PERSON FOR A TIME, AND OF THE CORONATION
OF OUR SOVEREIGN LORD AND ESTABLISHING OF
THE GOVERNMENT OF THE REALM IN THE PERSON
OF THE REGENT DURING HIS HIGHNESS'S
MINORITY.

At the accomplishing of this sudden and improvised marriage and council held in the afternoon preceding, few of the noblemen were present, as an act of such solemnity and importance had been requisite, for many of them finding themselves so trapped by coming to supper, and consequently by subscribing the bond the 19 day of April, fearing to be burdened with more ungodly and unlawful things, departed quietly and came not again to court but withdrew them to their houses secretly, to see what end that strange and marvellous confusion would draw unto, judging it rather better so to do than to offer true counsel where it was wilfully rejected and mocked at, as they trusted at the sight of the Queen's consent to subscribe the said bond on the said nineteenth day, and by her mocking when the noblemen sent to Dunbar offering to relieve her.

It is true that few nobles attended the marriage. The fact is, of course, that many of them had already, on 1 May, entered into an undertaking to 'liberate' Mary from Bothwell.

Hereafter divers means were made to draw the noblemen (that she and her feared disliked that state) to the court, where if they had come either they should have gone forward in all ungodly things with them or else have been warded or as well appeared destroyed and put to death. The hard conditions proposed to the noblemen that desired to pass out of the realm were a forewarning of the order devised for them.

This statement is not substantiated by either the Register of the Privy Seal *or the* Register of the Privy Council, *except possibly an ordinance of 22 May to the effect that, as it was impossible for all the nobles of the council to be permanently at court, four named groups of nobles were allotted to service for one quarter of the year each. Such an arrangement was not unprecedented, as the ordinance itself states. The only licence to leave the realm recorded at this point is one to Alexander, Bishop of Brechin, who received a protection in normal terms.*

So the circumstances of this whole tragedy gravely considered by divers noblemen how that wicked and godless man had found such fortune, in so ungodly a matter as by the murder of the king to obtain the Queen's marriage and government of the realm, besides the care of their own lives, which evidently they saw subject to evident peril and destruction. But most of all taking regard to the preservation of the innocent person of the native prince, whose life had not endured, his father's murderers having such authority, seeing it that is aspired to and obtained by wicked means, by the same means customably it is maintained. Therefore the said noblemen and other good subjects driven to the uttermost point of just necessity behoved to take arms on the sudden, thinking nothing more godly nor more honourable in the sight of the world than by punishing of Bothwell, chief author of the murder, to relieve others unjustly calumnied thereof, to put the Queen to liberty and freedom out of the bondage of that tyrant who so presumptuously had enterprised to ravish and marry her, whose lawful husband he could not be, neither she his lawful wife, and to preserve the innocent person of their native prince out of the hands of him that murdered his father, as well appeared by their proceedings at their coming near Borthwick, out of the which, how soon they knew Bothwell to be escaped, they showed no kind of pursuit against the Queen be passed back to Edinburgh, there to advise on their great and weighty purpose and to give warning to the remaining noblemen of their occasion of their taking of arms and intention to proceed to the punishment of the murder.

As already mentioned, the lords opposed to the Queen and Bothwell had entered into their first bond on 1 May. It is hard to reconcile the intention to 'liberate' the Queen with the earlier statement that she had been carried off with her own consent.

And Bothwell, knowing the noblemen and their company to be departed towards Edinburgh, sent the laird of Ormiston into Teviotdale, one that was present in person at the King's murder, with his other friends, and by them caused the Queen to be convoyed from Borthwick to the castle of Dunbar, arrayed in such form that it was marvellous to the beholders at that time and unworthy presently to be rehearsed, ever thinking by her and her authority to cover him from punishment.

Mary was at Borthwick from 7 to 11 June, and left for Dunbar in male attire.

Soon after coming to Dunbar, which was Wednesday at night the 11 day of June 1567, strict proclamations passed forth, commanding all men to repair in warlike manner towards the Queen and Bothwell, then termed Duke of Orkney, her husband, whom convening he marched from Dunbar on Saturday the 14 day, having in his company, besides the power of the country,* carted ordnance and hired men of war. Wherefore the noblemen convened for pursuit of the murder being too late advertised removed out of Edinburgh and upon Sunday the 15 day approached to the said Earl's company, which then was at Carberry Hill, 15 miles from Dunbar and five miles only from Edinburgh, where, being enquired of the cause of their taking of arms, declared the occasion to be the pursuit of the murder of the King upon the Earl Bothwell, chief author thereof, for indeed the quarrel was then only intended against him and the remaining known murderers, without the bloodshed of any innocent man, and in token thereof it was offered to try the matter with him in single combat between the companies according to the law of arms by a gentleman undefamed, whose name being enquired the laird of Tullibardine declared him ready thereto. But the murderer Bothwell shifting (against the tenor

* I.e., the local levies.

of his challenge which or before he had proclaimed) said he would fight with any earl or lord on the other party. The Lord Lindsay accepting the condition prepared himself immediately for the same, and the most part of both the companies looked assuredly to have seen the matter then instantly tried. But the murderer despaired of his quarrel and, moved by the grudge of his guilty conscience, not without the Queen's persuasion, refusing all, escaped by flight to Dunbar Castle, incurrring thereby the ignominy due unto the vanquished by the law of arms. And she, preferring his impunity to her own honour, would see him convoyed away. And to the end he should not be followed nor pursued came herself to the noblemen assembled against the murderer, who convoyed her to Edinburgh.

This account is substantially in agreement with all other accounts of the events at Carberry.

And being in Edinburgh upon the 16 day of the said month of June 1567, albeit her inordinate favour shown to the said Bothwell, her husband's murderer, was too great a presumption to convince her as guilty of the murder, yet the noblemen passed to her, humbly requiring her that she would see the murderers punished and be content that the pretended and unlawful marriage wherein she was imprudently entered to be dissolved for her own honour, the safeguard of her son and the quietness of her realm and subjects, to the which no other answer could be obtained but rigorous menacing on the one part, avowing to be revenged on all them that had shown themselves in that cause, and on the other part offering to give over the realm and all, so that she might be suffered to possess the murderer of her husband. And in farther proof of her indurate affection towards him she convoyed a purse with gold to him by David Kintore the same 16 day, which her inflexible mind and extremity of necessity compelled the noblemen to sequestrate her person for a season from the company and having intelligence with the said Bothwell and his favourers until farther trial might be taken and execution made for the murder, seeing it had been impossible to make any punishment therefor, she remaining at liberty and her passion suffered to work its own effect.

The allegation that Mary was prepared to give up all in order to follow Bothwell echoes the statement that she had said she would follow him over the world in a white petticoat.* While in Edinburgh, Mary was closely guarded, and it is not easy to believe that she succeeded in communicating with Bothwell.

The noblemen remaining at Edinburgh earnestly travailing by

* P. 53 above.

143

enquiry and otherwise to have the said murderer tried and punished, Bothwell, then admiral of the realm, abiding a certain space at Dunbar, repaired to the north land, and there prepared to pass to the sea in piracy as the last trade that wicked and desperate persons commonly frequents. And yet sent to the castle of Edinburgh for a box with letters which he left there, thinking if he could have the same the ground of the cause should never come to light. But as God willed the box was intercepted and taken from the deceased George Dalgleish, his servant, and being examined there was found in the same such letters of the Queen's own handwriting directed to the said Earl and other writings as clearly testified that as he was the chief executor of the murder so was she of the foreknowledge, counsellor, deviser and maintainer of the authors thereof, and that her ravishing preceding her pretended marriage with the said Earl was nothing else but a coloured masque invented and commanded by herself, as a cloak of the abusing of her body and filthy life frequented with him of a long continuance, both before and after the murder of her husband.

This statement is the official version of the discovery of the Casket. It is reasonable to believe that Bothwell wanted to gain possession of his title-deeds to his dukedom, as well as to Liddesdale and Dunbar, and according to Morton's account of the finding of the Casket these deeds were in it. But it appears that Bothwell had his letters patent of Orkney with him when he arrived in Norway. That Bothwell took to piracy is confirmed by a complaint of a citizen of St Andrews whose ship was seized by him in July.

Which strange and unnatural cruelty before suspected being now evidently known by many infallible proofs and arguments was openly spoken of among the people and so the fame thereof at last came to the Queen's own ears, whereupon, considering her former ungodly life and wicked behaviour and how just occasion she had given to her subjects to mislike and weary of her government, she was content to demit and resign the same with her royal crown and all pertinents thereof in favour of her son, now our sovereign lord, and during his minority to establish the regiment of the realm in the person of the Earl of Moray, without his knowledge or desire, he being then absent out of the realm, and that voluntarily, no compulsion, violence or force in word or deed used or practised to move her thereto.

No indication is given here that Mary abdicated under constraint, probably threatened with execution if she refused and ultimately yielding to the physical force of Lord Lindsay's hands.

7. The Enquiry: The Conclusion

The conference at Westminster had ended with the withdrawal of Mary's commissioners and the presentation by Moray of the Book of Articles, the Casket Letters and other evidence. After this the proceedings in the 'great cause' moved into their final phase, when the English government was mainly concerned to stage a performance designed to impress those who did not look too closely into what had gone before. The scene was changed to Hampton Court, and additional weight was given to the English representation. On 14 December the privy council, at Elizabeth's command, called on another half-dozen earls – Northumberland, Shrewsbury, Huntingdon, Westmorland, Worcester and Warwick – as 'principal persons of the nobility of England', to hear a narrative of the events at York and Westminster. An account was given to them of the whole proceedings, concluding with 'the last session, ended about the 10th instant'. Next day, the Book of Articles was read to this illustrious gathering, along with certain other productions of Moray, and the earls were then told that they had now been made participant of the whole cause but were reminded that the Queen had charged them to keep it secret. Elizabeth was obviously anxious to carry her notables with her in the course she was following, and, while nothing was said about Mary's counter-accusations against Moray, a statement was made to the earls which amounted to a defence of Elizabeth's refusal to give Mary an audience:

'Where the Queen of Scots' commissioners, being made privy to this accusation of the said Queen, have forborne to answer to the same, refusing also to have any further conference in this matter, pressing only to have the Queen, their mistress, permitted to come to the presence of the Queen's Majesty to make her answer, and otherwise to make no answer at all – it has been considered by Her Majesty, and thought not unmeet in this sort following to answer the said commissioners, if they shall persist in their said request: That Her Majesty will be very willing and desirous that some good answer may be made by the said Queen either by her commissioners and delegates or by her own self, before such sufficient persons as Her Majesty would send to her; but, considering Her Majesty had at her [Mary's] first coming into the realm found it not meet for her own honour to have her (being so commonly defamed of so horrible crimes) to come to her presence before she might be thereof some way purged, so also now, the crimes (wherewith she has been by common fame burdened) being by many vehement allegations and presumptions, upon things now produced, made more apparent, she cannot, without manifest blemish of her own honour in the sight of the world, agree to have the same Queen to come into her presence until the said horrible crimes may be by some just and reasonable answer avoided and removed from her – which Her Majesty would wish might also be.'

This had the intended effect, and the earls agreed that their Queen's attitude was justified.

Fortified by the assent of the earls, Elizabeth could now make a formal reply to Mary's commissioners. This she did at Hampton Court on 16 December, in presence of the Lord Keeper, Norfolk, Northampton, Sussex, Bedford, Leicester, Clinton, Howard, Cecil, Sadler and Mildmay. Addressing Lesley, Boyd, Herries and Kilwinning, she took up the 'motion of appointment' or proposal for a compromise which they had made on 4 December and their refusal to engage in further conference if Mary were not allowed to appear before her. She repeated what she had said on the 4th, namely that she had thought it more meet to have Mary's subjects reproved for rebellion than to make her answer in person, and she had therefore caused her commissioners to rebuke Moray and his associates. The latter had replied that in self-defence they must accuse Mary, and had done so, by producing 'such matters . . . as are very great presumptions and arguments to confirm the common reports against the said Queen'. Elizabeth said that she would now reopen the hearing if Mary would give a direct answer either by sending a trusty person or persons with power to make it, or by answering in person to such noblemen as Elizabeth would send to her, or by appointing either her late commissioners or others to make answer before Elizabeth's commissioners. She repeated the reasons she had given to her earls on the previous day for her refusal to receive Mary. The latter's refusal to answer, she pointed out, was the surest way to procure her own condemnation, and she hoped Mary would acquit herself by some reasonable answer.

These displays on 14 and 16 December achieved two objects. In the first place, the most influential men in England had now been made fully cognisant of the evidence against Mary, but her defences had not been put before them. Secondly, responsibility for the breakdown of the conference had been thrown on Mary's commissioners, and the implication was presumably intended that Mary's refusal to answer sprang from inability to put up a convincing defence.

In a sense the conferences had ended in a deadlock, but it was not quite as Elizabeth represented it. The difficulty was that Mary would make no promise to answer Moray's productions until she had examined them, whereas Elizabeth would not let Mary examine them until she had promised to answer them. The determination of both sides to adhere to their positions on this issue was many times reiterated. In letters to Knollys and to Mary on 20 and 21 December, Elizabeth repeated the substance of what she had said to Mary's commissioners, recounted the sequence of events from the appearance of the 'Eik', said that the conference had been 'stayed' pending an answer from Mary, and urged Mary to make an answer. Meantime, on 19 December, Mary had instructed her commissioners to ask that she should have copies of the writings which had been produced and that they themselves should insist on seeing the principals. Mary had seen a copy of the 'Eik', but apparently of no later production, and although her commissioners had a sight of the Book of Articles, they were denied a copy. On 7 January Mary declared to her commissioners that she would defend herself and accuse her enemies if she could have the writings they had produced, or at least copies thereof. Again, on 11 January, Mary's commissioners repeated their complaint that they had not yet seen the evidence, and on 13 January the English council considered Mary's request to have 'such letters and other writings wherewith she is charged'. It was explained to Mary's representatives that Elizabeth did not mean to deny Mary the sight of true copies of the writings, but before delivering them she wanted Mary to appreciate that after they were handed over Mary would have to make her answer, without further objection about not being admitted to Elizabeth's presence; once Mary had answered, she would be proved either innocent or guilty of the crimes of which she was as yet merely accused, and if she did not prove herself innocent, then the Queen of England could never with honour show her any favour. That was the end of the *impasse* over the production of the documents and Mary's refusal to answer, and this last debate, on 11 and 13 January, actually came after Elizabeth had delivered her finding on the 10th, as we shall see.

But, while the formal proceedings may be said to have ended in this deadlock, it is obvious that both inside and outside the formal encounters of the three parties a good deal of re-thinking was going on, and it was from such re-thinking that the final settlement emerged. These developments are exceedingly complex, and to present them in a chronological framework would not be helpful, or even possible. It is better to glance first, briefly, at the chronology, with some recapitulation, and then discuss the various ideas which were shaping the situation. The 'Diary', as we may call it, is as follows:

20–21 December: Letters from Elizabeth to Knollys and to Mary.

22 December: Memorandum by Cecil envisaging the detention of Mary in England.

24 December: Meeting of Lesley and Herries with Norfolk, Northampton, Leicester, Howard and Cecil.

25 December: Lesley and Herries received by Elizabeth.

26 December: Discussion between Knollys and Mary, reported to Elizabeth and Cecil on 26 and 31 December and 1 January.

28 December: Meeting of Mary's commissioners with Norfolk, Leicester and Cecil.

2 January: Letter from Mary to her commissioners.

7–8 January: Meeting of Lesley and Herries with Elizabeth.

10 January: Elizabeth's 'sentence'.

11 January: Meeting of Moray and his colleagues with Lesley, Herries and Kilwinning.

12 January: Licence to Moray to leave London.

13 January: Meeting of English council.

31 January: Licence to Mary's commissioners to leave.

The most important development, clearly, was the growing conviction, among the Englishmen who had been informed of the recent proceedings, that Mary was guilty. Elizabeth had given a lead when, in her statement to Mary's commissioners on 16 December, she said that Moray's new evidence constituted 'very great presumptions and arguments to confirm the common report against the said Queen'. Cecil's memorandum of 22 December indicates quite plainly that he saw no possibility of Mary's being cleared of the charges against her – though in this there may have been an element of wishful thinking. When Knollys subsequently had an interview with Mary, and found her 'in her old humour of denial to answer', he said that he did not marvel that she was not disposed to answer formally, and thought her wise in taking that attitude, for 'it passed my capacity to see how by just defence she could disburden herself of the crimes that are laid against her'. To this Mary replied that she could answer her accusers. 'Well,' said Knollys, 'your grace had need to look about you, for you do stand in a very hard case . . . If you shall deny to answer (as you have good reason thereto), thereby you shall provoke the Queen my mistress to take you as condemned, and to publish the same to your utter disgrace and infamy.' And so, as he reported, he began 'to strike as great fear as I could'. Mary said, 'I am sure the Queen will not condemn me hearing only mine adversaries and not me.' 'Yes,' said Knollys, 'she will condemn you if you condemn yourself by not answering.' If this was discouraging to Mary, it was equally discouraging when, a couple of days later, Lesley, Herries and Kilwinning conferred with Norfolk, Leicester and Cecil and learned that their judgements were almost confirmed in favour of Mary's adversaries, 'notwithstanding our reasons to the contrary'.

Yet Mary's refusal to answer in the circumstances laid down by Elizabeth did not arise from any lack of spirit. On 19 December she wrote to her commissioners, mentioning that she had seen the 'Eik' and characterising the accusations made by Moray's party as lies, 'imputing unto us maliciously the crime whereof they themselves are authors, inventors, doers and some of them proper executors'. She claimed that the allegation that she had hindered investigation and punishment of Darnley's murder had been sufficiently answered at York, and to the charge that she had shown an unnatural attitude towards 'her only child' by intending 'to have caused him to follow his father hastily' she made a good retort by observing that such a charge came unfittingly from those who, in the Rizzio murder, 'did him wrong in our womb, intending to have slain him and us both'. When Lesley and Herries had their interview with Norfolk and others on 24 December, they said that they were authorised by Mary's letter to them of the 19th to accuse Moray and his party and to defend Mary's innocence, and when they saw Elizabeth herself the following day they produced the same defence and counter-accusation. Again, Mary told Knollys in their interview on the 26th that she could answer her accusers. Even on 11 January, the day after Elizabeth had given her finding, Moray and his colleagues challenged Lesley, Herries and Kilwinning as to whether they would accuse them of the murder. The latter said that they were commanded by Mary to do so, though they declined to proceed to specific accusations until they had seen Moray's evidence.

It is plain, too, that there must have been an awareness that Mary, allowing that she was really guilty, was nevertheless capable of putting up a strong defence, for only so can we explain the persistence, even at this late stage, of efforts to reach some kind of compromise. This was the burden of Cecil's memorandum of 22 December, in which he envisaged the detention of Mary in England and the bringing of James to England for his education. Mary, he thought, should be urged to accept such a settlement for a variety of reasons. For one thing, if, as he thought, Mary's guilt should be proved by further proceedings, Elizabeth would be bound to notify it to the world; and even if Mary was right in saying that Moray's party had been accessories to the murder and to the Bothwell marriage that did not extinguish Mary's own guilt. Besides, Elizabeth could not forget Mary's claim to the throne of England and could not allow her to leave the realm until 'she has repaired the wrong done by her claim to the crown'. Mary should be brought to see that, if she were restored, the Hamiltons and their dependants 'in blood', like Huntly and Argyll, would be in control, and neither Mary nor her child would have 'long continuance', whereas she would be safe in England and if James were brought to England it might be beneficial to 'her supposed title to this crown'. A letter from Elizabeth to Knollys of the same date intimated that 'on further consideration this is thought of all devices best for us' – that Mary should agree voluntarily that James should be King and Moray Regent, that Mary should remain in England 'during such time as we find convenient', that James, for his safety, should be brought up in England 'under persons of the birth of Scotland', and that 'this whole cause of hers whereof she hath been charged to be committed to perpetual silence'. When Knollys interviewed Mary on the 26th, four days later, he was probably aware of the drift of Cecil's and Elizabeth's thoughts, for he urged Mary to be content with the demission of her crown to her son and her own continued residence in England for 'a convenient time', and he pointed out the advantages of an English education for James. Maitland of Lethington, besides, ever dominated by hopes of Anglo-Scottish union, and ready as ever for a compromise, also produced a 'device' at this stage. He argued that Mary, in abdicating in favour of James, had not meant to deprive herself of the crown: 'she is determined', he said, 'to die a Queen, and yet for motherly affection wishes it shall not be derogatory to her son's estate'; therefore, he added, should James

die in her lifetime she would immediately return to the full enjoy-
ment of her own right, for 'this was her meaning from the beginning'. Any of the compromises or 'devices' which were under
consideration would, of course, have freed Elizabeth from the need
to pronounce any sentence.

However, Mary, still professing confidence in her ability to
defend herself, would have nothing to do with a compromise which
would look like an admission of guilt. When Elizabeth saw Lesley
and Herries on 7 January, she proposed an 'appointment' whereby
Mary should demit the crown and live in England. Lesley said she
would make no such demission, and declined even to convey such
a suggestion to his Queen. He had good reason for his attitude,
since Mary had already answered such a proposal by anticipation,
in a writing in which she requested 'the person who wrote her to
resign to trouble her no more with such a request, for she is
resolved to die rather than do it, and the last word in her life shall
be that of a Queen of Scotland'. On 8 January, therefore, Lesley
and his fellows rejected the suggestion Elizabeth had made on the
previous day, and asked for an arrangement whereby they could
come before the English council to declare plainly their mistress's
mind.

In the opinion of Knollys, who by this time knew Mary as well
as any Englishman did, the whole approach to Mary, both in
asking her to answer and in proposing a compromise, was badly
handled. When he wrote to Elizabeth reporting his interview with
Mary on 26 December, he gave his opinion that she was likely to
be 'stiff and unpliant' and declared that her stiffness should be met
with stiffness. In a letter to Cecil he repeated that 'the way of
winning of this Queen to conformity [i.e., agreement] is to use her
stoutly when she is backward, and to use her courteously when she
is pliant'. Five days later, on 31 December, he repeated to Cecil:
'If Her Majesty could handle the matter stoutly and roundly, she
would yield, in hope or assurance that she [Elizabeth] would save
her honour and use her favourably; but if the Bishop [Lesley] and
the others find her Majesty tender and shrinking in dealing with
her, or in supporting Moray thoroughly, then I look not for her
yielding.' Elizabeth's ways were much too devious to permit of
proceeding 'stoutly and roundly', and Knollys wrote to her the
next day saying that Mary was in fact optimistic as a result of
what she had gathered from Lesley:

'She saith that Your Majesty plainly said unto the Bishop of Ross
not only that you would have her a Queen still but also that Your

Majesty liked well that my Lord of Moray should take the execution of the government at the hands of her and her son jointly. Until the Bishop is sent away in despair, Your Majesty will never bring her to a resolute yielding, for she hath courage enough to hold out as long as any jot of hope may be left unto her. Till she sees a severe order for her removing she will believe in the Queen's mildness . . . The Queen is half persuaded that Your Majesty will not openly disgrace her nor maintain Moray, howsoever she refuses to conform . . . The which if Your Majesty have said it is too late to call it back again. But she looks for more favour than this comes unto.

It seems that, whatever impression may have been made on English ears by Elizabeth's carefully staged displays, the tortuousness and length of the negotiations were fraying the nerves of some of the Scots. On 22 December Lord Lindsay, one of Moray's commissioners, wrote to Herries saying that he lied in his throat in accusing Moray's party of the murder of Darnley, and offering to meet him in a duel. Herries replied that he had not mentioned Lindsay by name, but added: 'That you were privy to it, Lord Lindsay, I know not: and if you will say that I have specially spoken of you, you lied in your throat.' But he offered to take up a challenge from any of the 'principals', by whom he probably meant Moray or Morton. If the Scots generally were feeling the strain, to their nerves and also to their pockets, of being so long away from home, this was especially true of Moray himself. He had long been concerned about the possible effects in Scotland of his unexpectedly long absence: his passport, originally issued on 12 September for three months, had had to be extended in December, but he must have wondered how he was going to be recouped for the expense of his long residence in England. When Elizabeth wrote to Knollys on 20 December, she said that Moray's party had made 'earnest requests to know our further pleasure' and she had answered that, as there was no answer from Mary, she could not make any final determination of the cause, and was therefore ready to give Moray liberty to depart, without prejudice to his cause, leaving representatives who could make a further answer should a reply come from Mary. But, she explained, 'finding him not disposed to return without some final resolution, which also we can not justly make without her answer to some purpose, and yet understanding how perilous it is for his state to continue longer from his country, we are indeed desirous to have some answer from that Queen and without delay'.

It is unlikely that pressure from Moray or his anxiety to return to Scotland had anything to do with stimulating Elizabeth into delivering what passed for her sentence. The likelihood is that the idea had crystallised that Mary should be detained in England without either acquittal or condemnation. The inference from Cecil's memorandum of 22 December is that Mary's detention should be the solution, without her acquiescence if she would not agree to remain voluntarily, and he even argued – on grounds unknown – that Mary was 'a lawful prisoner by treaties'. Such a solution resolved many problems, not the least of which was mentioned to Elizabeth by the Earl of Arundel on 4 January: 'One that has a crown can hardly persuade another to leave her crown because her subjects will not obey. It may be a new doctrine in Scotland, but it is not good to be taught in England.' A paper of 7 January assessed the possibility of so dealing with Mary as to keep her in England without passing judgement; it was an obvious step to turn to this when Mary refused to demit the crown and reside in England of her own volition, but it was still intended to gain her acquiescence: 'whatsoever shall be determined, that the same may be obtained to proceed of the Queen of Scots as of herself, without any open note of compulsion'. It was intended that she should 'require licence to remain in this realm, free from the troubles of the government of her realm', while James remained King and was brought up in England and the government of Scotland rested in the hands of Moray. Mary would retain the title of Queen, but the government would be carried on in the name of James. Alternatively, James and she might be in name joint sovereigns, while Moray directed the government. The Scottish parliament, it was suggested, might legislate to this effect, with penalties on Mary should she break the conditions imposed on her and with power to Elizabeth to act as 'defender of the said ordinance'. To induce Mary's consent to this, she must not understand that Elizabeth meant to deal no further in the matter because Mary refused to answer the accusations against her. Moray was to return to his regency 'in no worse state than she [Elizabeth] found him at his calling from thence.

These thoughts led straight to the 'sentence' of 10 January 1569. It was in Elizabeth's power to make a decision whether or not she had Mary's acquiescence and on 10 January there was announced her inconclusive finding which is usually regarded as marking the end of the enquiry which had been going on intermittently for three months. In the presence of the commissioners and the council, Cecil made 'such answer in effect as follows':

'Whereas the Earl of Moray and his adherents came into this realm at the desire of the Queen's Majesty of England to answer to such things as the Queen, their sovereign, objected against them and their allegations: forasmuch as nothing has been deduced against them as yet that may impair their honour or allegiance, and, on the other part, there had nothing been sufficiently produced nor shown by them against the Queen their sovereign whereby the Queen of England should conceive or take any evil opinion against the Queen, her good sister, for anything yet seen, and there being alleged by the Earl of Moray the unquiet estate and disorder of the realm of Scotland now in his absence, Her Majesty thinks meet not to restrain any further the said Earl and his adherent's liberty but suffer him and them at their pleasure to depart; relinquishing them in the same estate in the which they were of before their coming within this realm, till she hear further of the Queen of Scotland's answers to such things as have been alleged against her.'

The final peculiarity of those strange proceedings is that the sentence, insofar as it was a sentence, was not pronounced by the court, if there had ever been a court. Indeed, the 'sentence' is not extant in any official account, and is preserved only in Bishop Lesely's narrative, but its general accuracy, at least, is vouched for by the fact that two days after it had been delivered, namely on 12 January, Moray and his party were given licence to depart for Scotland. The Regent was able to leave with a sense of satisfaction, for there was no doubt that, despite the apparently equal treatment given by Elizabeth to him and to his Queen (both of whom were in effect pronounced innocent), he was substantially the victor. On 14 January he was authorised to buy eighteen horses, two dozen long bows of yew and two dozen sheaves of arrows. On the same day Elizabeth wrote to the wardens of the marches instructing them to ensure the safe transit of Moray and his party, to aid the Regent in every possible way and not to allow any Scotsman to enter England without Moray's special recommendation. Better still, on 18 January Moray gave a receipt for £5,000 lent to him by Elizabeth in his great necessity 'for the maintenance of peace and resisting of the common enemies of both realms', to be repaid in two instalments, on or before 24 June and 1 November following. Moray was still in London on 19 January, but at the end of the month he wrote to Cecil from Berwick acknowledging that he had been 'honourably convoyed' on the English side of the Border, and there is no doubt that, while the 'sentence' had been to the effect that Moray's 'estate' was to be unchanged, his government was now in effect recognised by England.

Besides, while the 'sentence' had implied that both parties were innocent, they were differently treated. Moray was given liberty to depart for Scotland, but when Mary's representatives said that if he had a licence to go she should have one also, no such licence was given, and they had to be content with a protest that if she were detained in England that should not prejudice her. On 2 February, some days after Moray had left London, when Lesley and Herries appealed afresh for permission to Mary to leave for Scotland, Elizabeth replied that she had taken on her 'the order and redress of her causes' and, as this task had not yet been perfected, she could not let Mary go. The prospect of Mary's continued detention had inevitably led to a revival of talk of her going to France, and as late as 16 December Mary's representatives had asked that if Elizabeth would not restore Mary or allow her to return to Scotland she would at least allow her to pass to France, but Elizabeth's answer had been that she would give no reply to their request until Mary had said that she would reply to the accusations. The mention of France had, however, probably been no more than a matter of form, and nothing was said of such a possibility after Elizabeth had given her 'sentence'.

That Mary herself might be allowed to leave England was evidently never seriously entertained. As we have seen, the idea of detaining her was far from being a new one, for Sussex had written so early as 22 October, 'I think surely no one can be made good for England except the person of the Scots Queen be detained, by one means or another, in England', and two months later Cecil, in one of his memoranda, had said much the same. So far as can be made out, the ultimate decision was arrived at almost tacitly, without any formal discussion, but of course it must have become evident that, if Mary were not going to be sent back to Scotland to meet her fate there, and was not going to resign her crown voluntarily, her detention in England was almost the only possible course.

However, although Mary herself was to remain in England, the question of the departure of her commissioners had to be settled. On 21 January Lesley and Herries asked for leave to go, but requested that two of Mary's commissioners should remain with her as long as she was in England. On 31 January they were licensed to leave, but on the same day Moray, writing to

Cecil from Berwick, remarked, 'If the Lord Boyd, Herries the Bishop of Ross could be stayed for a season, it would do great good'. This suggestion can hardly have reached London on 2 February, when Elizabeth agreed that, while Mary should retain two of her commissioners, safe-conducts should be granted to Livingston and Boyd to depart for Scotland, visiting Mary on their way. Elizabeth caused a letter to be given to them, in which they were accredited to the Queen of Scots, 'and pleasantly demitted them; and so they took their leave humbly of Her Majesty'. Mary had arrived at Tutbury on 4 February, and ten days later the Earl of Shrewsbury, her keeper, reported that she 'continues very quiet in outward behaviour, and talks only of indifferent matters, with mild and seemly words when Elizabeth is mentioned'. Boyd and Lesley, he added, were in Burton, three miles off, where he reported, 'I think they mean to linger, and I shall watch for them'. Despite his suspicions, Elizabeth ordered that Boyd and Lesley should be allowed to 'tarry about' Mary.

There was also the allied question of Châtelherault, who had been hovering ineffectively in the background all this time. On 7 January, remarking that he had remained in London at the desire of the English ambassador for sixteen weeks, far beyond his expectation, he asked for permission to leave for Scotland. By 4 February he was at York, and wrote from there mentioning that his necessity in London had been well enough known to the goldsmiths in Cheapside, to whom he had had to sell some 'sober silver plate' in order to meet his expenses. The Commendator of Kilwinning, who, while nominally on Mary's commission, was really representing the Hamilton interest, was allowed to leave London with Châtelherault, but was forbidden to call on Mary on his way north.

A complication had arisen which did a good deal to embitter relations in the latter stages of the enquiry. This emerged from some of the proposals for an 'appointment', which could only too easily be represented as likely to lead to undue English influence in Scotland. It was to Mary's interest to foster reports of this kind, and as early as 9 December she started to circulate rumours which went far beyond anything which, so far as we know, had actually been proposed. By that time she was, as she said, in despair of any satisfactory issue from the enquiry, and concluded that although Elizabeth had indicated that she proposed to examine Moray for his conspiracy so that there should be 'some happy outgait [outcome] to my honour and contentment', this had not in fact been 'the butt she shot at, for my matters have been prolonged in delays'. Meantime, she added, 'my rebels practise secretly' to deliver the prince to the English and hand over the castle of Edinburgh, Stirling and Dumbarton, while Moray would remain in control and would be declared heir to the throne after Mary and James and any descendants of the latter, with a view to holding the realm as an English vassal. She also had a story of a pact between Moray and the Earl of Hertford (who, like Moray, stood close to the royal line, though through marriage) whereby the one was to succeed in Scotland and the other in England. On 17 December Mary wrote to the Earl of Mar, keeper of Stirling Castle and guardian of her son, warning him of English designs.

The English government was disturbed by the rumours, and on 22 January there was a proclamation, drafted by Cecil, denying 'slanders' that James was to be brought to England, that Edinburgh and Stirling Castles were to be occupied by English garrisons, that Dumbarton (then held for Mary) was to be besieged and taken for England, that Moray was to be legitimated so that he could succeed, failing James and his descendants, and hold Scotland as a fief of England. These reports were characterised as 'absolutely false and devised of mere malice and rancour'. On the same day Elizabeth wrote to the Earl and Countess of Mar reassuring them of her intentions towards James, and she also wrote to Knollys asking if Mary would deny the accusations against Elizabeth which were being circulated in her name in Scotland. Mary retorted, on 28 January, by writing to Cecil accusing Moray's creatures of circulating the offending documents and falsely attributing them to her.

Mary was naturally inclined to make the most of the reports which the English authorities characterised as 'slanders', and it was appropriate to turn them to account as propaganda at a time when she was beginning to encourage her supporters in Scotland to renew their resistance to Moray. Her letter of 9 December was little less than a mainfesto, winding up with a message urging her friends to rally against the regent, and on the following day she wrote to Lord John Hamilton (Châtel-herault's second son and leader of the Hamilton interest in his father's absence) and the rest of her supporters, begging them to assemble their forces and prevent the return of Moray and the other leading 'rebels' from England. On 5 January she wrote to the Earl of Huntly, and it was as part of the same campaign that she had drawn up the 'Declaration of Huntly and Argyll', which is written in the same hand as the letter to Huntly. This 'Declaration', prepared for the earls' signature, with blanks for date and place of singing, was intended as part of an attack on Moray and his party as conspirators against Darnley. Evidently it, like the letter to Lord John Hamilton, was intercepted, and Moray prepared a reply to it on 19 January. Mary wrote further to her supporters to stimulate them to renewed activity, on 18 January, but this letter too was intercepted.

Although so many of Mary's letters were intercepted, there is no doubt that her party in Scotland was fully informed of her situation and of the alleged nefarious designs of the English government and of Moray, for at some date in January Argyll, in Mary's name, issued a proclamation reciting the rumours and summoning the lieges to arms to resist England and the English agent, Moray. One result, therefore, of the English decision to detain Mary was the ending of the armistice which had begun when the enquiry at York opened, and the resumption of civil war in Scotland. Mary's cause, which had impressed those in England who heard it fairly presented, was cogent enough to make an influential body in Scotland fight for it for three more years.

8. Epilogue: Towards the Second Trial

The inconclusive 'sentence' of 10 January 1569, which few contemporaries can have regarded as in any way definitive, left almost everything unsettled. So far as Mary's prospects were concerned, it was to be shown again and again that the door to her restoration to the Scottish throne had by no means been finally closed. Within six months her supporters in Scotland were putting forward for consideration by the estates there a proposal that she should be divorced from Bothwell as a preliminary to her restoration – and also to her marriage to Norfolk. Negotiations for her restoration were revived from time to time throughout the whole period of her captivity, and there were two phases in which they were not unrealistic – in 1569–70 and again between 1581 and 1584. Equally, she had not made any resignation of her claim to the English throne, and there had not even been a decision by the English government against her rights as Elizabeth's heir. Finally, she remained as attractive as ever as a possible bride for ambitious suitors, whether on the continent or in England. Before the proceedings at Westminster were even over there were signs of the resumption of intrigues for a continental marriage, for on 3 January 1569 Bishop Lesley, writing to the Earl of Arundel, mentioned that the King of Spain had empowered his ambassador to offer three possible marriages – with Philip himself (who had become a widower again in 1568 by the death of Elizabeth of Valois), with the Archduke Charles or with Don John of Austria, Philip's half-brother.

However, if all else remained unsettled, some arrangements had at least to be made for the conditions in which Mary was to continue to live in England, whether temporarily or permanently. On 20 January Elizabeth wrote to her, remarking that her affairs were 'not so clear as they should be'. This was an implied threat against an accused and unacquitted prisoner, and it was the background for the remarks which followed it in Elizabeth's letter:

understanding, so she said, that Mary disliked Bolton, she had prepared another place for her and had ordered Knollys and Scrope to escort her there. Word of a likely removal had evidently come to Mary's ears before that letter was written, for on 21 January Henry Knollys (who was acting in place of Francis, as the latter was distracted by grief at the death of his wife) informed Cecil that Mary had said she would not remove 'without violence', and he added the sinister remark, 'But we shall know the certainty this night'. Next day Mary wrote to Elizabeth, reproaching her for refusing to see her and for detaining her. What follows is not a pretty story. It was on the 26th that Mary was taken from Bolton, 'with an evil will and much ado', and reached Ripon. While subjected to this experience, she was meantime being pressed to repudiate the 'slanders' of which the English government complained – that is, the allegations that England was going to establish control over Scotland – and 'refuseth them plainly for none of hers', but, Henry Knollys reported next day, 'we forbore troubling her thereon last night for her weariness after the journey and late arrival at her lodging'. On the 28th Francis Knollys added that Mary did not deny that four of the first lines' of an offending letter were agreeable to a letter she had indeed sent concerning Moray's promise to deliver her son to the English. She also admitted that she had issued a proclamation to stir up the people against Moray, but denied that any of the slanderous parts touching Elizabeth were hers.

Meantime, the Earl of Shrewsbury, Mary's new keeper, had received his instructions as to the treatment of the captive. She was to be treated as a Queen, with reverence fitting her degree and her nearness in blood to Elizabeth. On the other hand, he was to beware lest she try to gain influence over him or attempt to escape, and no one was to be in her company save her retinue and others who received special permission. From 1569 until 1585 Shrewsbury continued to be Mary's custodian, and she spent her time mainly at Sheffield Castle, with only the occasional intermissions which the sanitary conditions of the time dictated and a visit now and again to Buxton for the sake of her health. She was treated with the formal respect due to a Queen, sitting under a royal cloth of state and appointing the members of her own household. The expenses of the establishment were borne by the English government. At the same time, Mary's own person and her surroundings were far too closely guarded to admit any possibility of escape without external assistance in force. All her correspondence, too, was supposed to pass through Shrewsbury's hands. However, Mary had a sufficient income from her revenues as Queen Dowager of France to ensure that means could be found to maintain secret contact with English Roman Catholics and with plotters on the continent, and she was fertile in ideas for conveying letters surreptitiously. She became an inveterate plotter, and as the years went by and her declining health made her less able for hunting and other outdoor recreations, embroidery and intrigue were her chief occupations. Yet only too often her agents were beaten by the intelligence service of Elizabeth's government and her supposed secrets were discovered. Her brother-in-law, Charles IX of France, remarked in 1572 with some prescience: 'Ah, the poor fool will never cease until she lose her head. In faith, they will put her to death. I see it is her own fault and folly. I see no remedy for it.'

It is hard to acquit her of folly when one reflects that her situation from 1569 onwards was not necessarily less happy than her return to Scotland would have been. Had she gone back to Scotland as Queen, whether under formal limitations or not, she would inevitably have had to depend on some faction and would therefore have been subject to limitations in practice. It was remarked several times, and Mary herself must have realised it, that there was no faction in Scotland which would put her interests before its own. Cecil may have been exaggerating when he said, more than once, that if she went back neither she nor the prince would 'have long continuance', but the danger was there, as had been abundantly shown in the past. The Englishmen who met the Scots at York took as poor a view of them as Cecil did. Sussex had said in his letter of 22 October that the two factions 'for their private causes, toss between them the crown and public affairs of Scotland . . . and care neither for the mother nor the child (as I think before God) but to serve their own ends'. And Norfolk said that many of the Scots sought wholly to serve their own private ends, caring not 'what becomes of either King or Queen'. Cecil returned to his argument later: Mary, he said, should be brought to see that if she was restored, the Hamiltons and their dependants, like Huntly and Argyll, would be in control, and neither she nor her son, he repeated, would 'have long continuance', whereas she would be safe in England. Englishmen may have been too ready to sneer at the politics of their neighbours, but a Scot whose attitude was fair and detached said much the same: 'some drew to both the factions that desired never to see either King or Queen in an established estate'. Perhaps Mary was better out of it all. Was it really in her interest to face the possibility of a repetition of the Rizzio, the Darnley or the Bothwell episode? It would have been quite reasonable to calculate that she might do better to remain in England and exploit her claims to build up a party which might in the end win two kingdoms for her.

It has to be remembered, too, that Mary was not yet, in 1569, publicly defamed in England. When Shrewsbury received his instructions for her detention he was told to warn her that, if she made trouble or if she uttered any speeches about Elizabeth's actions toward her which reflected on Elizabeth's honour, it might cause the English Queen to publish 'her whole causes and doings to the world'. This was a threat, but it was also a promise, and might well have been an incentive to good behaviour. Although the accusations against her had been made known to a good number of Englishmen, they had not been published, and none of the proceedings had been public. No doubt reports circulated, and there was even a certain amount of material in print. Robert Sempill's *Ane Declaratioun of the Lordis Just Quarrell*, published in Scotland in 1567, gave the case against Mary, partly on constitutional arguments but partly on her immorality, and John Pickeryng's *Horestes*, a play presented at the English court late in 1567, had been transparently an account of Mary's doings under the guise of Clytemnestra. But as long as Mary acted with some discretion Elizabeth kept her promise not to give official authorisation to the publication of the case against her. Not only so, but when 'French Paris', the one-time servant of Bothwell, was arrested and examined in Scotland in August 1569, Elizabeth pleaded for the deferment of his execution so that he could be more fully examined in the hope that the truth would emerge; but the government of Moray had caused him to be executed before Elizabeth's plea arrived. It would seem that Elizabeth was not entirely acting a part when she withheld judgement on Mary and refused to have her formally condemned. As we shall see, it was only after the revelations of Mary's implication in the Ridolfi plot of 1571 that Elizabeth released the evidence against the Scottish Queen.

Mary's prospects, and the schemes which in one way or another concerned her, were all along closely linked with the international situation and affected by its changes. Right at the outset, indeed while the enquiry was still going on, events had taken a turn which, it seemed, might work to her advantage. At the end of 1568 Elizabeth had seized money destined for the Spanish forces in the Netherlands, after the ships carrying it had put into English ports to escape pirates. Alva, the governor of the Netherlands, retaliated by seizing English ships and goods. It looked as if there must be war between England and Spain, which would surely, so Mary thought, mean the landing of a Spanish force in England, on which she counted to overthrow Elizabeth and set her up as Queen of England. Nothing came of this, and indeed no serious Spanish attempt was ever to be made at the invasion of England until after Mary was dead, but the possibility was never long absent from her mind.

It was also true that, as Cecil had foreseen, Mary almost at once became the focus of plots within England itself, though these plots were nearly always linked with proposals for collaboration with France or Spain and the papacy. The fact is that, if the decision of 1569 could in some ways be interpreted as being to Mary's advantage, it is hard to see that it brought much gain to Elizabeth. Undoubtedly by holding Mary and being able at any time to threaten to release her, Elizabeth acquired some influence over the Scottish government; but this was a meagre advantage to set off against the constant anxiety to Elizabeth and the constant stimulus to English plotters which arose from the presence of a rival Queen within Elizabeth's own realm.

In the first phase, in 1569, Mary's cause was supported by a very mixed band of conspirators, some of whom wanted the restoration of Roman Catholicism, some of whom aimed merely at ending the ascendancy of Cecil and some perhaps simply at avoiding the perils of a disputed succession by securing the recognition of Mary as heir to the crown. Mary had so many well-wishers in England at this point – many of them admittedly for purely selfish reasons – that one feels the force of Elizabeth's refusal to publish the evidence against her, as well as the results of the activity of her defenders, notably John Lesley, whose *Defence* of Mary was printed in 1569. One of the roots of the plotting in England was the projected marriage to Norfolk, which had never been lost sight of after it was first mooted at York in October 1568. In the marriage itself there would have been nothing either unreasonable or traitorous towards Elizabeth, especially as Norfolk was not a Roman Catholic and indeed had a strain of puritanism in his upbringing, but in the eyes of those who pressed it it was clearly intended to involve Mary's restoration to Scotland and her recognition as Elizabeth's heir, and the conservative peers who associated with Norfolk saw it as a means of wresting power from Cecil and the ultra-Protestant and anti-Spanish interest. Beyond this, however, lay the activities of the northern earls, Northumberland and Westmorland, who carried their conservatism to the extent of planning the restoration of Roman Catholicism, if necessary with foreign help, and their schemes were incompatible with the continuance of Elizabeth's rule or even of her life. Mary was in touch with this group as well as with the more moderate men, including for a time Leicester, who aimed primarily at the displacement of Cecil. Elizabeth weaned Leicester from the conspiracy and tried to detach Norfolk, but the Duke failed to respond and found himself in danger of being drawn to lend countenance to armed revolt. This he refused to face, so he obeyed a command to come to court and was sent to the Tower on 11 October 1569.

Norfolk, Mary and the Spanish ambassador all advised the northern earls against action, but when Elizabeth summoned them to court the result was the outbreak of a rebellion, in November. The rebels made for Tutbury to release Mary, but she was hurried off to Coventry before they arrived, and they were afraid to risk venturing beyond Yorkshire. The midlands and south of the country provided ample levies of loyal forces to counter theirs, and, faced with the certainty of defeat, they broke up without a serious battle. Their leaders crossed the Border into Scotland, but over 500 of their humble followers were put to death.

The Earl of Northumberland was held a prisoner by Moray, who tried to bargain the surrender of the Earl in return for financial assistance and full recognition of his regime. Before Elizabeth could come to terms, Moray was murdered (23 January 1570). The situation led to English intervention in Scotland, of a somewhat peculiar and limited nature. The Earl of Sussex and Sir William Drury conducted military operations to punish Borderers who had harboured fugitives from the late northern rebellion and to despoil the lands of some of Mary's Scottish supporters. Elizabeth also used her influence with the Scottish leaders to have the Earl of Lennox, Darnley's father, appointed as Regent (July). But Elizabeth had intervened in these ways with a view less to extinguishing Mary's hopes in Scotland than to creating conditions in which she could be restored under strict limitations. In the negotiations that followed we see the significance of the fact that the Marian party in Scotland included not only some of the most influential magnates but also some old friends of England, among them now Maitland of Lethington, who appealed to Elizabeth for Mary's restoration within the context of the maintenance of the Anglo-Scottish *entente*. Elizabeth favoured Mary's restoration at this point partly with a view to neutralising France and preventing that power from intervening in Scotland on Mary's behalf. Cecil was sent to negotiate with Mary, and representatives of the King's party were summoned from Scotland. The latter came, early in 1571, but were far from enthusiastic, for they felt their own position incompatible with Mary's restoration on any terms. They made the excuse that they must first consult a parliament, which was due to meet in May. Before anything further could be done, events happened which altered Elizabeth's attitude to Mary and put her restoration out of the question for a long time.

Elizabeth's relations with Roman Catholics, both at home and abroad, had entered a new phase with the papal bull excommunicating her, issued in February 1570 and brought into England in May. On top of this came the Ridolfi plot. Ridolfi, a Florentine banker who had carried on business in London, had acted as a papal agent and had dealt with the Spanish ambassador and with Lesley on behalf of Mary. He was one of the many over-credulous or over-optimistic Roman Catholic agents who could sketch harebrained schemes and assume that foreign powers and English and Scottish magnates would be so reckless as to commit themselves without reservations and without guarantees. Again and again foreign armies of 10,000, even of 20,000, men were conjured up with an ease that there was nothing to justify, and a quite insignificant agent could speak as if their landing in England, Scotland or Ireland were a certainty. Some of these agents were far more dangerous to their friends than to their enemies. At this stage, Norfolk, released from the Tower but under surveillance and sworn not to deal further for a marriage with Mary, had in fact remained in touch with her and also with Lesley, though probably not traitorously and quite possibly with a view to exercising a restraining influence. Yet he was to some extent drawn into the plot, though not as far as Ridolfi and Lesley represented. Ridolfi's plan was for the landing of a Spanish army sent by Alva from the Netherlands and a simultaneous rising by Norfolk and the English Roman Catholics. Ridolfi went to the continent in March 1571 to complete the arrangements, armed mainly with grossly over-optimistic assessments of the situation in England and the attitude of Mary and Norfolk. He found that Alva was cautious and was disposed to insist that the English rising must precede the invasion. Letters were intercepted, the whole thing was discovered, and Cecil made the most of it, in the first place to discredit Norfolk. The Duke was arrested and tried for treason, on the grounds of his attempts to marry Mary, a rival claimant to Elizabeth's throne, the assistance he had given to refugees from the northern rebellion, the fact that he had remitted some money to Mary's supporters in Scotland and his part in a conspiracy for the deposition of Elizabeth with foreign help. Tried with the characteristic injustice of English treason trials of the period, Norfolk was convicted. He admitted that he had received a letter from the Pope, but insisted that he had never written to the Pope and that if a letter had gone in his name it must have been a forgery. After prolonged hesitation on the part of the Queen, Norfolk was executed (2 June 1572). John Lesley, who had long been regarded with suspicion by the English government, had also been arrested, and had made admissions which went a long way to incriminate his mistress.

It has become something of a fashion to contend that all the Roman Catholic conspiracies in England, from Ridolfi's to the Gunpowder Plot, were fabrications by the English government, designed to discredit the Roman cause or sometimes merely to bring about the downfall of some individual. Mary's experience had already shown, and was again to show, that fabrication and trickery could be resorted to, and there is, besides, clear evidence that some adventurers were so lacking in loyalty to either Mary or Elizabeth that they could be brought either by bribes or threats to play double parts. It is also true that the animosities between different factions of the Roman Catholics were such that accusations of disloyalty were somewhat freely made. The inexplicable thing is that the plotters placed any confidence at all in men who were not wholly above suspicion. However, reviewing the history of half a century, not only in Britain but on the continent, there is such ample evidence of papal encouragement for revolution and assassination that neither Mary nor the English Roman Catholics seem cast for the parts of injured innocents. In this case, quite apart from what Lesley, Mary's agent, disclosed – admittedly under conditions of strict imprisonment in the Tower – papers found when Dumbarton Castle had been captured from Mary's supporters in April 1571 provided evidence of her dealings with Alva.

After this episode, Elizabeth not only abandoned the current negotiations for Mary's restoration, but she withdrew her opposition to the defamation of Mary and permitted the publication of incriminating matter. Before 1 November 1571 the Latin text of Buchanan's *Detectio* was printed in London, with, appended to it, a Latin *Actio contra Mariam* and three of the Casket Letters. The *Actio* had been written by Thomas Wilson, later secretary of state. Wilson translated the *Detectio* and the *Actio* into what he called 'Scottish', and added all eight Casket Letters. This publication, as *Ane Detectioun*, appeared in two editions, within a month of the Latin original. Meanwhile a genuinely Scottish edition of the *Detection* had been printed at St Andrews, and there were editions in Germany and France. It was only with the issue of this hostile publicity that Mary, for the first time, stood before the world publicly indicted as a murderess. No such public indictment had emerged at the time of her first trial.

If Elizabeth was prepared to authorise these publications, her subjects were ready to draw the inferences. Already in a parliament before the Ridolfi revelations, there had been a bill which in effect took away from Mary and her heirs any title to succeed to the throne of England. Now, in 1572, when parliament met again, members clamoured for the execution of Mary, as well as for that of Norfolk. Mary, it was declared, had 'heaped up together all the sins of the licentious sons of David, adulteries, murders, conspiracies, treasons and blasphemies against God'; she had instigated the rebellion in the north and had practised with Ridolfi for the invasion of England. The influence of the *Detectio* is surely to be seen in the exclamation of one member that she was the most notorious whore in all the world. But if Elizabeth was so reluctant to take the final, irrevocable step with her own subject, Norfolk, she was not likely to approve of the execution of a sister queen. Not only so, but a bill, which passed both houses, declaring it treason to support Mary's title to the English crown, providing for her trial by the English peers if she plotted against Elizabeth again and authorising her death without trial if any insurrection took place in her favour, was denied the royal assent.

There was, however, another possible way of dealing with Mary, and that was to send her back to Scotland to receive justice there. An essential preliminary to any such move was to come to terms with France. That country might have been expected to act in Mary's favour, but a by-product of the Ridolfi Plot, exploited to the full by Cecil, was the revelation that Mary was depending on Spain and not on France. This facilitated the making of the Treaty of Blois, concluded between England and France in April 1572 and making no reference to Mary. In the following August the massacre of St Bartholomew's Eve raised the hopes of Mary's supporters, who saw the possibilities if France adopted a militant anti-Protestant policy abroad as well as at home; but its more important effect was to embitter English feeling against Mary and at the same time to encourage Elizabeth's resolution to bring about a settlement in Scotland before France might intervene there. In September and October Elizabeth contemplated handing Mary over to the Scottish government, but after the death on 28 October of the Regent Mar (who had succeeded Lennox in September 1571) English policy was directed instead to bringing about a settlement in Scotland without reference to Mary at all. The fact was that Elizabeth was less moved emotionally by the massacre than her subjects were, and she saw no reason in the long run to alter her policy of keeping Mary still in detention in England, but still alive. In 1573 English artillery was sent to Scotland to reduce Edinburgh Castle, the last stronghold of Mary's supporters, and the war between the King's Party and the Queen's Party came to an end. The Earl of Morton was now Regent, and as long as his rule endured there were no prospects for Mary in Scotland.

On the international front, too, there was a period which was less eventful and less encouraging for Mary, because there was a kind of uneasy equilibrium. English Roman Catholic refugees on the continent agitated for action against Elizabeth, and the Pope, too, was eager that Roman Catholic sovereigns, especially Philip of Spain, should take up 'the Enterprise of England' as a crusade. But Philip feared that war with England might involve him in war with France as well, and he knew that action by him against Elizabeth would stimulate her assistance to his rebellious subjects in the Netherlands. At the same time, if Spanish action in England were in favour of a French Queen-Dowager, it might be hard for France actively to oppose a Spanish expedition. However, Elizabeth's own diplomatic skill, combined with Philip's caution and the reluctance of his governors in the Netherlands to allow troops to be withdrawn for an attack on England, maintained something like peace.

The most promising situation for Mary at any time between 1573 and 1580 arose after 1576, when Don John of Austria, Philip's half-brother, became governor of the Netherlands. Something of a European hero after his victory of the Turks at Lepanto in 1571, but still under thirty years of age, he seemed the ideal leader for another crusade, this time against heretical England. The general idea was that after making peace in the Netherlands he would invade England, free Mary and rule the country as her consort. But Don John's success in the Netherlands was never so complete as to make the Enterprise of England opportune, and Philip, cautious as ever, did not long give his full support to the project. Yet for a year or two fears and hopes centred on Don John, and when he died in October 1578 Elizabeth's ministers thought it a salutary miracle.

The final phase of the intrigues involving Mary may be said to begin in 1580, for from that point until her death plot succeeded plot, and conspiracy was almost incessant until the climax which led to her second trial and her execution. In a general way, the situation was shaped by a heightening of the militancy of papal policy. For some years Roman Catholic missionaries had been reaching England from the seminary at Douai, and in 1580 they were reinforced by the more dedicated and aggressive Jesuits. This activity led to a fresh wave of alarm and anger in England, and not without reason, for the missionaries rallied the English Romanists and put an end to the possibility that they would be quietly and gradually absorbed into the Church of England. To make matters worse, a papal pronouncement was issued in 1580 that anyone assassinating Elizabeth, 'with the pious intention of doing God service, not only does not sin, but gains merit'. The practical outcome of such a policy was illustrated in two attempts to murder William of Orange, the leader of the Protestants in the Netherlands, the second of them successful (1584).

By 1580, too, events in Scotland had taken a turn which offered possibilities both of a base being found there for the Enterprise of England and also of the restoration of Mary to the Scottish throne by negotiation. The regency of Morton, who had excluded former Marians from office, came to an end in 1578, and this opened the question, in many minds, of what influences were going to shape the policy of King James (now twelve) as he emerged from tutelage. Morton did not finally lose control of affairs until the end of 1580, but already there had been established in Scotland a faction, or at least an interest, which was disposed to challenge every aspect of Morton's policy – his antagonism to Mary, his resolute adherence to Protestantism, and his constancy to an English alliance. The opposition to Morton found a leader in Esmé Stewart, a first cousin of Darnley, who arrived from France in September 1579 and rapidly won the devotion of the adolescent King, who created him Earl and subsequently Duke of Lennox. Esmé's real objectives were most likely personal and dynastic – he was, after a childless great-uncle, the King's nearest kinsman on his father's side – and there is no reason to believe that his arrival in Scotland was designed as a move in a Roman Catholic enterprise. But there were those who thought they could use him in the papal interest.

Mary herself took some initiative by proposing, through the Duke of Guise, a 'scheme of association' whereby she should be restored as joint-sovereign with her son. This proposal, which was revived in various forms over the next two or three years, seemed on the face of it to have much to commend it. To James it offered a degree of formal recognition which could never be forthcoming otherwise as long as his mother lived. To Elizabeth it offered the prospect of settling the problem of Mary and, provided that the terms were sufficiently firm and faithfully carried out, rendering her innocuous. To Mary, who was not likely to believe that her sovereignty could be restricted, it was, of course, merely a stage towards the recovery of real power. James might have accepted the scheme provided Mary remained in England, and Mary at one stage professed to be ready to do so – but only so that she would be available to join a Roman Catholic army of invasion when one came. It is doubtful, in fact, if the interests of the various parties could have been reconciled.

But those who thought they could use Lennox in the Roman Catholic interest included the usual band of credulous and optimistic priests, this time the English Jesuit Parsons and two Scottish Jesuits, Crichton and Hay, who worked closely with the Spanish ambassador in London, Mendoza. Glowing reports appeared that not only Lennox but some of the leading Scottish earls would accept Spanish help to bring about James's conversion or, if he refused, to depose him. Early in 1582 an ambitious, but quite unrealistic, scheme was hatched: a large force was to be sent from the continent, Lennox would put himself at its head and, after securing Scotland, would raise the Roman Catholics in England. As Mendoza put it, in a letter to Philip, Mary was 'virtually the mainspring of the war, without whose opinion and countenance Lennox and others will do nothing'. James himself showed an opportunism worthy of his mother in her more diplomatic days: he wrote to her in polite terms, he also wrote to Guise, and he interviewed some of the clerical emissaries in secret. His position was far too insecure to enable him to take a strong line, and he calculated that his equivocal attitude might be a reinsurance should Spain take the Enterprise up seriously and carry it through with success.

Lennox, whether justly or not, was denounced in Scotland as an agent of the counter-reformation, and in a *coup d'état* known as the Ruthven Raid (August 1582) was displaced by an ultra-Protestant faction who controlled the King for ten months. He withdrew to France and died there the next year. Elizabeth had remained more or less neutral in relation to Lennox: after all, he represented French influence, and at this stage England was so closely allied with France that the Queen was renewing her dalliance with the French King's younger brother. She was probably right not to be stampeded by her ultra-Protestant advisers into action against one whose ecclesiastical standpoint was at worst equivocal and who was associated with her ally, France, rather than with Spain. It was quite logical, therefore, that she was almost equally neutral towards the Ruthven Raiders, strongly pro-English though they were, and declined to subsidise them on the scale they craved. No only so, but she continued to toy with the idea of an 'association' of Mary with James.

When James escaped from the Ruthven Raiders in June 1583, he inevitably had to rely for a time on a more conservative element which was favourable to Mary. He went so far as to correspond with Guise, and even wrote to the Pope early in 1584. It was only to be expected that, at Mary's instance, plans for the Enterprise were revived, though the proposal was now for a landing in England rather than in Scotland. However, as James began to feel increasingly secure in Scotland, he had less need to seek continental support, and other factors soon diminished his enthusiasm for any kind of continental entanglements. After June 1584, when the Protestant Henry of Navarre became heir to the French throne, the Guises were more fully occupied at home in organising opposition to the succession of a heretic king. Besides, the Spaniards, who had never been enthusiastic for a restoration of Mary through French agency, now took up the Enterprise more wholeheartedly. It was evident that Philip was unlikely to conquer England merely in order to hand it over to James, the latter therefore became more ready to come down firmly on the English and Protestant side. This meant abandoning the cause of his mother, and early in 1585 he categorically repudiated any intention of approving of the 'association' of Mary with him. In May 1585 a league between Scotland and England was formulated, and it became a binding treaty in July 1586. Mary's claims were quietly ignored.

Mary herself had continued to negotiate energetically with Spain, though Philip and his advisers were beginning to have doubts about conquering England even for her, since her heir was a heretic. Mary ultimately disinherited her son and made over her rights to Philip, but apparently not until May 1586. Meanwhile, the idea had taken shape, in the minds of the most zealous English Roman Catholics as well as in those of the Spaniards, that Philip should ignore James and Mary alike, but conquer England and then claim a right to its throne in virtue of his own descent from Edward III. But the Spanish negotiations were highly detrimental to Mary's position. In November 1583 Francis Throckmorton, who had acted as her agent in her intrigues with Spain, was arrested, and under torture revealed her secrets. Various English nobles and gentlemen who had been involved either fled when they heard of his arrest or were imprisoned. In January 1584 Mendoza, the Spanish ambassador, was dismissed from the English court. In

October 1584 the Jesuit Crichton was captured, with papers which revealed more details of the Enterprise.

These events, combined with the assassination of William the Silent in July 1584, led to an outburst of feeling in England against Mary which it was beyond Elizabeth's power to check completely. In October the English council drew up a Bond of Association, which pledged its signatories to contest the succession of any person in whose interest an attempt should be made on Elizabeth's life and to kill that person by any means in their power. The Bond was widely signed. In November parliament proposed to authorise it by statute, and all Elizabeth could do was to secure the insertion of a modification to the effect that, should Mary become liable to death under the terms of the Bond, she must first be proved to have been an accomplice to the plot and must be formally tried before being put to death.

In January 1585 Mary was moved to Tutbury, with a new gaoler, the unyielding puritan Sir Amias Paulet, and with a much stricter regime which stopped her secret post. At the end of the year Gilbert Gifford, a Roman Catholic sent from the continent to try to reopen communications with Mary, was arrested on landing and agreed to play the spy for Walsingham by opening a channel for Mary's correspondence which she would think secret but which would be tapped. On 24 December Mary was transferred to Chartley, where the trap was set. The household received its beer from Burton, and the brewer who supplied it was induced to convey letters to and from Mary in a waterproof packet inserted through the bung-holes of the casks. But every letter that passed was intercepted and copied for Walsingham before being forwarded. The system began to operate in January 1586, and Mary, overjoyed to have a means of communication open to her for the first time for a year, launched into voluminous correspondence.

A few months later, without initial reference to Mary, a band of English Roman Catholics, headed by Anthony Babington, formed a plot for the assassination of Elizabeth as the essential preliminary to any sucessful invasion from abroad. When Babington disclosed the plot to Mary and she – quite possibly instigated by a double-dealing agent – replied with a letter which eagerly welcomed it, Walsingham pounced without delay, and Mary's papers were seized. Babington and his fellow conspirators were executed in September. The council wanted to have Mary sent to the Tower, but Elizabeth decided on Fothinghay, where in October her second trial began, before thirty-six peers, privy councillors and judges, for having compassed or imagined acts tending to the hurt of the Queen. Mary's protest that she was no subject of Elizabeth was set aside, but she defended herself with dignity, courage and skill. She admitted that she had attempted to gain her freedom with the aid of foreign powers, but denied having sought the Queen's life or even of having corresponded with Babington. Her original letters could not, of course, be produced as evidence, for after being copied they had been forwarded, but Babington himself, as well as Mary secretaries, admitted the accuracy of the copies. Even if the evidence of the copies were not admitted, and even if the evidence by word of mouth had been obtained by threats or by hopes of favour, Mary's own admissions in effect went far enough to condemn her, for no one could have believed that Elizabeth would not die in the event of a successful foreign invasion. Mary was judged guilty, and a few days later parliament petitioned for her immediate execution.

Elizabeth then entered the final phase of her persistent irresolution towards Mary. She asked parliament if some other way could be found, short of the death sentence, but the unanimous answer of both houses was in the negative. Even after the death-warrant was signed, on 1 February 1587, Elizabeth tried to persuade Paulet, as a signatory to the Bond of Association, to take it upon himself to despatch his prisoner, but he was too scrupulous to agree. Even then Elizabeth hesitated, but her secretary, William Davison, took the warrant to the privy council, who on their own responsibility sent it off. Mary was beheaded on 8 February.

NEL BESTSELLERS

T011 682	ESCAPE ON VENUS	*Edgar Rice Burroughs* 40p
T013 537	WIZARD OF VENUS	*Edgar Rice Burroughs* 30p
T009 696	GLORY ROAD	*Robert Heinlein* 40p
T010 856	THE DAY AFTER TOMORROW	*Robert Heinlein* 30p
T016 900	STRANGER IN A STRANGE LAND	*Robert Heinlein* 75p
T011 844	DUNE	*Frank Herbert* 75p
T012 298	DUNE MESSIAH	*Frank Herbert* 40p
T015 211	THE GREEN BRAIN	*Frank Herbert* 30p

War

T013 367	DEVIL'S GUARD	*Robert Elford* 50p
T013 324	THE GOOD SHEPHERD	*C. S. Forester* 35p
T011 755	TRAWLERS GO TO WAR	*Lund & Ludlam* 40p
T015 505	THE LAST VOYAGE OF GRAF SPEE	*Michael Powell* 30p
T015 661	JACKALS OF THE REICH	*Ronald Seth* 30p
T012 263	FLEET WITHOUT A FRIEND	*John Vader* 30p

Western

T016 994	No. 1 EDGE – THE LONER	*George G. Gilman* 30p
T016 986	No. 2 EDGE – TEN THOUSAND DOLLARS AMERICAN	
		George G. Gilman 30p
T017 613	No. 3 EDGE – APACHE DEATH	*George G. Gilman* 30p
T017 001	No. 4 EDGE – KILLER'S BREED	*George G. Gilman* 30p
T016 536	No. 5 EDGE – BLOOD ON SILVER	*George G. Gilman* 30p
T017 621	No. 6 EDGE – THE BLUE, THE GREY AND THE RED	
		George G. Gilman 30p
T014 479	No. 7 EDGE – CALIFORNIA KILLING	*George G. Gilman* 30p
T015 254	No. 8 EDGE – SEVEN OUT OF HELL	*George G. Gilman* 30p
T015 475	No. 9 EDGE – BLOODY SUMMER	*George G. Gilman* 30p
T015 769	No. 10 EDGE – VENGEANCE IS BLACK	*George G. Gilman* 30p

General

T011 763	SEX MANNERS FOR MEN	*Robert Chartham* 30p
W002 531	SEX MANNERS FOR ADVANCED LOVERS	*Robert Chartham* 25p
W002 835	SEX AND THE OVER FORTIES	*Robert Chartham* 30p
T010 732	THE SENSUOUS COUPLE	*Dr. 'C'* 25p

Mad

S004 708	VIVA MAD!	30p
S004 676	MAD'S DON MARTIN COMES ON STRONG	30p
S004 816	MAD'S DAVE BERG LOOKS AT SICK WORLD	30p
S005 078	MADVERTISING	30p
S004 987	MAD SNAPPY ANSWERS TO STUPID QUESTIONS	30p

NEL P.O. BOX 11, FALMOUTH, TR10 9EN, CORNWALL

Please send cheque or postal order. Allow 10p to cover postage and packing on one book plus 4p for each additional book.

Name ....

Address..

....

Title ....
(SEPTEMBER)